OFFENDER MOTIVATION & VALUES: HIGH SPEED ISSUES IN INTERNATIONAL SECURITY

JOHN ROBERT CENCICH, J.S.D.
EDITOR

THE HAGUE PRESS INTERNATIONAL

Library of Congress Cataloging-in-Publication Data
Cencich, John R., 1957 –
    Offender Motivation and Values /John R. Cencich (ed.)
    260 Pages cm (studies in crime and public policy)
    ISBN 978-0-991329328
        (paperback)
    1. Federal Bureau of Investigation *Law Enforcement Bulletin*.
    2. International Security. 3. Kidnapping.
    3. Criminal behavior. 5. Crime. I. Title.

Printed in the United States
The Hague Press International
First Edition

CONTENTS

INTRODUCTION

By

John Robert Cencich, J.S.D.

FOR ALL TOO LONG, THE ART AND SCIENCE OF POLICE work has largely been reactive. The police and other law enforcement agencies typically respond to reports of crime and endeavor to locate the perpetrators and have them prosecuted successfully in court. In many respects, the tragic events of 9/11 changed this method of operation (MO) and standard operation procedure (SOP)—not only for the police—but also in the world of international security.

International security is a notion that means different things to different people. In many ways it is a component of a larger concept known as human security, which the United Nations has called upon its member states to embrace.[1] Such a broad precept embodies the security of food and water, poverty reduction, and health issues.[2] It also includes urban crime, human trafficking, and man-made disasters such as the placement and remnants of landmines.[3]

The notion of international security also encompasses the safety and security of international civil servants, members of nongovernmental organizations (NGOs), and many others who must travel abroad for any number of reasons. Indeed, in many ways this conceptualization overlaps with several of the specifically enumerated categories of human security recognized by the United Nations.

But how do we ensure the safety and security of the global population and the men and women who risk their lives daily in the pursuit of such an endeavor? From the perspective of criminal and similarly serious threats, domestic police agencies are not always positioned or trained to provide the specific type of security or training for their citizens that intend to travel abroad or for those who enter the sovereign borders of their country.

On the other hand, traditional security personnel often do not possess the type of experience that is gained by police officers throughout their careers and which is often crucial to the success of the mission. This includes the ability to sort issues out on the spot, skill in dealing with people from all walks of life, knowledge and understanding of different cultures, and how to cultivate and handle confidential informants.

In my view, it is a combination of the security and law enforcement talents that maximizes strategic and operational success. I have found that professionals who possess relevant *interdisciplinary* knowledge, skills, and abilities are ideal in the field of international security. Alternatively, similarly designed *multidisciplinary* teams work well. To be sure, teamwork is almost always an integral ingredient for such undertakings.

As a special agent with the U.S. Air Force Office of Special Investigations (OSI), I was fortunate to have gained invaluable experience in both fields. For example, OSI's national and international security activities involve protective service operations (PSOs), counterintelligence and counter espionage cases, and national security investigations, including the exploitation and neutralization of terrorist threats. Criminal investigations are almost always focused on the most serious or major crimes such as murder, rape, robbery, and arson.[4] The Naval Criminal Investigative Service (NCIS) is the only other military criminal investigative organization (MCIO) that has this dual global mission.[5] The Federal Bureau of Investigation (FBI) does too, but it mostly works within the territory of the United States.

As I approached the end of my law-enforcement career, I was privileged and honored to have served a 4-year appointment with the United Nations International Criminal Tribunal for the former Yugoslavia (ICTY). Headquartered at The Hague in the Netherlands, my colleagues and I had a front row seat in the world of international security from two principal perspectives.

First, we saw the direct effects of what I will call human security transgressions. These included the plight and suffering of refugees and displaced persons, the presence of urban violence, widespread human rights violations, and a systematic pattern of violations of international humanitarian law, which included extermination, murder, torture, hostage-taking, sexual assault, cruel and inhuman treatment, exposure to antipersonnel landmines, and many other forms of persecution. Second, there was the omnipresent threat on the ground presented by ordinary criminals, anti-personnel mines, elements of organized crime, war criminals, foreign intelligence services, and military and political state actors who had a marked interest in our witnesses, evidence, and of course, ourselves.

With continued interest in international crime and security, upon returning to the United States I undertook doctoral-level research at the University of Notre Dame. My investigation sought, in part, to gain a better understanding of offender motivations and their behavioral manifestations in relation to international crime. Such an approach was undertaken with the view to developing new ways in which principal offenders of international crimes could be more effectively identified and prosecuted.

Still, this approach is reactive. Indeed, the United Nations recognizes the need to implement measures that are designed to *prevent* or minimize the occurrences of human security transgressions. Although many relevant steps have been effectuated, a lacuna in this area continues to revolve around the question of how behavioral analysis—in relation to violent crime—might assist in proactive measures related to critical matters such as hostage-taking, kidnapping, sexual assault, and assassination.

Consequently, the purpose of this book is to provide the reader with a better understanding of how behavioral criminology can indeed be used in international (as well as domestic) security situations. Such a relationship becomes readily evident when examining the motivation of offenders, and to be sure, actors that present potential risks in domestic or international security settings are indeed offenders. Having a better understanding of their motivations assists greatly in undertaking threat assessments and violence risk assessments.

In their efforts to ascertain the motivations of certain offenders (from a proactive perspective), members of the FBI's Behavioral Science Unit (BSU) utilize a research-driven, multi-step direct interview technique known as the "Perpetrator-Motive Research Design" (PMRD).[6] In fact, the BSU is currently undertaking a number of research projects that include international security-related topics such as hostage-taking, mass victimization, behavior in the cyberworld and emerging technologies, counterintelligence, and insider threats.[7]

What I have done in this book is taken a number of selected articles that will contribute to a better understanding of the socio-psychological aspects of offender motivation as relate to international security. While there are very few, if any, journal articles that address such issues, what you will see is a combination of papers on criminal investigation, behavioral analysis, and domestic and international security.

These articles come from both the FBI *Law Enforcement Bulletin* and publications of the National Institute of Justice. They are followed with critical thinking exercises and discussion questions that I developed. To the extent possible, I have interjected my own experiences in the exercises and questions. I will present dilemmas that I have personally been faced with. Sometimes I sorted the issues out, and there were times that I did not. But that is called experience, and there is nothing like personally understanding the struggles that police officers and international security specialists face on a daily basis.

But my experiences are not gratuitous "war stories." I weave my participation and observations into the teaching points. The first objective is to combine reality on the street with critical thinking and scholarship. This approach is followed by a secondary objective, which is to see how you might respond to some of these situations. Accordingly, we will examine your problem-solving thinking process as an individual, and more importantly, as part of a team.

ENDNOTES

---

[1] United Nations, General Assembly, *Human security: Report of the Secretary-General*, A/64/701 (8 March 2010), available from undocs.org/A/64/701
[2] Id. Paragraph 19
[3] Ibid.
[4] Air Force Office of Special Investigations, welcome page. http://www.osi.af.mil/main/welcome.asp
[5] Naval Criminal Investigations Service http://www.ncis.navy.mil/Pages/publicdefault.aspx
[6] Federal Bureau of Investigation http://www.fbi.gov/about-us/training/bsu
[7] Id.

PERSPECTIVE
THE DISEASE OF CERTAINTY
By Everett Doolittle, D.P.A.

March 2012: *FBI Law Enforcement Bulletin*

I HAVE HAD GREAT OPPORTUNITIES OVER MY MANY YEARS IN law enforcement. I have served as a police officer, a deputy sheriff, and even the chief deputy, but I found my greatest career opportunity at the Minnesota Bureau of Criminal Apprehension (BCA). At BCA, I tackled my most challenging assignment when I led the Cold Case Unit (CCU).

Early in my career, I gained valuable experience by working on homicide teams. But, studying the errors of others and reworking an old case granted me even greater insight into why cases fail. This article describes one of the major sources of these investigative errors: a phenomenon I dubbed the "Disease of Certainty."

The Disease of Certainty is fatal to investigations. Both inexperienced and seasoned officers can catch this contagious disease, and it can spread throughout a team. It occurs when officers feel so convinced of their own beliefs that they allow themselves to become tunnel-visioned about one conclusion and ignore clues that might point them in another direction. Those who resist the disease may be ridiculed and ostracized for their supposed lack of understanding and inability to see the truth if all of their coworkers share the same beliefs and assumptions about the investigation.

The numerous cases that CCU worked over the years taught us many lessons about the Disease of Certainty. For clarification, when I refer to the BCA CCU, I include all members of the BCA team (agents, analysts, forensic scientists, and support personnel) and the local and county investigators who assist these investigations. Cold case investigations demand a multiagency approach to solve a difficult problem, so a diverse set of personnel with varying expertise comprise the team.

By describing what I have learned about the Disease of Certainty, I do not aim to demean the work of the initial agencies involved, but to help others avoid the same mistakes in the future. I want to eliminate this deadly disease of perception that can prevent investigators from seeing beyond their own assumptions. All of these cases involved dedicated and professional individuals, but fatal errors occurred nonetheless. CCU does not aim to judge the initial investigators but to work with the agency as a team to reinvigorate the investigation. One person or agency never deserves all of the credit for cracking a case because it demands a true team effort.

A Case Study
My work with CCU began with numerous rape and assault cases, but I will focus on a series of homicides. The first of the confirmed homicides occurred in December 1978. As the Huling family slept in their secluded rural farm house north of the Twin Cities (St. Paul and Minneapolis) in Minnesota, an intruder entered their home. Before leaving, the intruder viciously murdered Alice Huling and three of her children—miraculously, one survived.

Several other seemingly unrelated crimes occurred over the following year. The next one took place in May 1979 when Marlys Wohlenhaus came home from school. A few hours later, her mother returned from errands and found Marlys severely beaten and unconscious. The girl was pronounced dead 2 days later. Next, in the following months, a young woman disappeared after leaving a restaurant. Though her car quickly was discovered near the Mississippi River, her body was not found for another 5 years. Yet again, soon after, a young girl left another restaurant where witnesses saw her forced into a vehicle, and her body was found days later.

These cases shocked the surrounding communities. However, because no apparent relationship existed between the crimes, the police departments investigated them individually. Several independent investigations continued for many years. In each of the cases, police identified a different prime suspect who became the central focus of the investigation.

The Disease Defined
To understand the seriousness of this issue, I need to explain the investigative process and how problems can arise. There are two logical approaches to problem solving that investigators must understand and use effectively: deductive and inductive reasoning. Deductive reasoning results from the evidence that people see in murder-mystery movies—the smoking gun, witnesses, DNA, fingerprints, and other tangible facts and clues. With deductive reasoning, this evidence builds the foundation of the case, and everything comes together to point to one conclusion.

Unfortunately, most real-life investigations differ greatly from the ones seen on television. In many cases, investigators can gather little if any tangible facts or evidence, which leads to a difficult, complex investigation that quickly can become a cold case. In these instances, investigators must turn to inductive reasoning to evaluate possible directions and outcomes. Through inductive reasoning, or scenario-based logic, we determine possibilities and probabilities based on experience and intuition and then attempt to prove or disprove them. Investigators start with a simple question, for example: Who killed Marlys Wohlenhaus? Could it be her boyfriend? What would be his motive? Could it be her stepfather or the neighbor kid who lives down the block? What would be their motives? Investigators attempt to identify possibilities and eliminate them one by one until only the most probable solution remains. To the seasoned investigator, this type of reasoning becomes the routine course of action.

These types of reasoning can go awry when in the mind of an investigator a possibility becomes the only reality. When officers become convinced of a certain solution, they may think that others who disagree with their answer simply do not understand. In most cases, experienced investigators' instincts are correct, and their prime suspect indeed committed the crime. Nevertheless, one always must keep an open mind to the facts that disagree with an initial assessment as probability does not equate to certainty. Anyone can come to an incorrect first conclusion, especially when little or no straightforward evidence exists, and a conclusion is based mainly on conjecture.

The Case Resolved
In the serial murders outlined above, this Disease of Certainty led law enforcement personnel to disregard key information because it did not agree with their previous conclusions. However, when CCU reopened the case, many new hypotheses developed, and answers were found among the volumes of information the initial investigators had gathered. As in many cold cases, this only could happen when some initial investigators were

removed and new personnel were assigned to support the case.

Eventually, CCU solved these crimes by examining a suspect who quickly had been cleared in the initial investigation. This man was not an acquaintance, stepfather, priest, or deputy, but a stranger. Joseph Ture was a drifter who lived in his car at a rest stop about 4 miles from the Huling home. Four days after the murders, police arrested Ture for an unrelated crime and found a ski mask, a club wrapped in leather, and a small toy car in his possession. These items became significant years later.

Two years later, in 1981, Ture was arrested and convicted of the murder of another waitress. While awaiting trial, he supposedly talked to his cellmate about his involvement in the murders of the Huling family and Marlys Wohlenhaus, and his statements were forwarded to law enforcement agencies. When officers questioned Ture, he maintained his innocence and claimed he was working at an automobile plant in St. Paul when the homicides occurred. The investigators contacted the plant and confirmed that a Joseph Ture was working on the assembly line at the time of the murder of Marlys Wohlenhaus. As a result, the officers eliminated Ture as a suspect.

When CCU personnel examined this case 20 years later, however, they reconsidered evidence, such as Ture's statements to his cellmate and the items he possessed at the time of his initial arrest. They double-checked Ture's alibi and realized that it actually was Joseph Ture, Sr., the suspect's father, who worked at the automobile plant at the time of the murder. Upon further inquiry, CCU members discovered other incriminating remarks that the suspect made to his cellmate. Ture divulged information that only someone with direct involvement in the crime would have known. Also, the team found that Billy Huling, the one surviving child of the Huling home, could identify the toy car found with Ture when he was arrested decades earlier; Billy and his brother, Wayne, had played with a similar one prior to the night their family was murdered.

This example illustrates how investigators can become too convinced of their own conclusions. Because Joseph Ture allegedly was working at the time of the Wohlenhaus murder, officers disregarded other significant evidence against him. Once CCU reexamined previously held truths about the case (such as Ture's alibi), they solved the crimes. This case has appeared numerous times on television.

Dangers of Overconfidence

Over the years, I have seen priests, deputy sheriffs, stepfathers, neighborhood kids, boyfriends, parents, spouses, and other innocent suspects become not only the focus of the investigation but the only possible answer in the minds of investigators. Once investigators develop this mind-set, it takes courage for others to stand up and disagree with the one perceived truth.

Also, this Disease of Certainty seriously can damage innocent individuals who mistakenly become the focus of the investigation. In some instances, little or no factual evidence exists against a suspect, yet the police, community, and media all believe the individual committed the crime. Rather than grieving the loss of a friend, acquaintance, or loved one, the suspect must deal with being viewed as a criminal in the eyes of the public.

Investigators face the challenge of pursuing their work confidently and proactively, yet understanding that they can be wrong and that if they are their errors impact many people. In this way, officers hold much power and influence over the lives of others, and their ethics matter a great deal. Police may want to solve cases quickly by relying on their instincts and investigating aggressively, but they also have a duty to remain open-minded, fair, and thorough. Working cold cases, I have seen the conflicts that arise when these priorities fall out of balance.

CCU's success in identifying Ture as the murderer in no way detracts from the competency of the original investigators. But, to combat the Disease of Certainty, agencies must remember that personnel assigned to a particular case do not "own" that investigation. In the serial murders described above, the initial investigative teams included experienced officers who had long records of success, yet their experience may have contributed to their failures. These errors, while understandable, may not have occurred had the investigators not formed such strong beliefs of who committed the crimes. Experienced investigators draw on their past successes, which may blind them to unexpected possibilities.

A Wide Perspective
Many of the cases worked by CCU, like the Wohlenhaus and Huling murders, involved talented and dedicated personnel who focused too narrowly on one hypothetical conclusion. One incorrect hypothesis should not jeopardize an entire case. Every investigation reveals several paths that can lead in any number of directions, and, if it dead-ends, investigators need to turn around and try a new one. Problems arise, however, when police venture down the wrong path and refuse to see that they are going in the wrong direction.

Once investigators develop this fixed mind-set, they filter out information that disagrees with their conclusion and only see the evidence that supports their answers. I have observed this phenomenon often while managing multiagency task forces and referred to it as the "Don Quixote Effect." Don Quixote, a famous literary hero, mistakenly battled windmills because he believed so strongly that they were giants. This idea resonates in Thomas Kuhn's 1962 book, The Structure of Scientific Revolutions, which discusses the difficulties experienced by scientists when they discovered information that disagreed with their long-held truths or paradigms.

Overconfidence is not the only way that the Disease of Certainty can infiltrate an investigation. Sometimes, a lack of perspective leads the team awry. When investigators dig deeply into the facts of a case, they can become too focused on one suspect, one lead, or one piece of information and lose sight of the bigger picture. This line of thinking caused investigators to mistakenly eliminate Joseph Ture as a suspect in the crimes described above.

When venturing into a densely wooded forest—it is easy to lose sight of the forest when surrounded by trees. Similarly, when officers become bogged down by puzzling information and unanswered questions, they may find it difficult to see the bigger picture of the case. Solving a difficult and complex investigation with keen inductive reasoning demands more than a team of dedicated personnel; it requires a leader. True leaders can see beyond disparate facts and seemingly unrelated evidence to view the whole "forest," and they have the courage to tell others when they are heading in the wrong direction.

Conclusion
Because the Cold Case Unit receives cases after a significant amount of time has passed and all initial leads have been exhausted, it brings a fresh perspective to the puzzle. CCU's investigators are not the same team of officers who responded to the scene of the crime, interviewed witnesses, interacted with a grieving family, and felt the pressure of media attention that surrounds

high-profile cases; because of this, they may provide a new approach missing from the initial investigation.

Additionally, because CCU receives cases that stumped a dedicated team of investigators, cold case officers know they must consider "out-of-the-box" solutions and, thus, are less susceptible to the Disease of Certainty. A unit, such as ours at BCA, can provide this service for any agency willing to challenge experienced investigators' long-held beliefs and dig into old cases. Agencies must remember that even their most talented officers can fall victim to overconfidence, and this Disease of Certainty may have caused errors in cold cases that still can be resolved.

DISCUSSION QUESTIONS

1. Hungarian Scientist Albert Szent-Gyorgyi said, "Discovery consists of seeing what everyone has seen and thinking what nobody has thought." How do you think such a statement fits with the "Disease of Certainty"?

2. Throughout the years I have encountered professionals and colleagues who speak in "absolutes," and often in connection with police work and criminal investigations. What is meant by this term, and what might be a good way to deal with such a person?

CRITICAL THINKING EXERCISE

The author of this article makes a very good point regarding the scientific investigative process, but there is much more to this than deductive and inductive reasoning. As a group, develop a short outline on the process to include how hypotheses are formed, and how inductive and deductive reasoning can be incorporated into the process. Be sure to provide short definitions of the terms that you use and how they apply to a criminal investigation.

VETTING CONFIDENTIAL HUMAN SOURCE INTELLIGENCE THROUGH INVESTIGATIVE STATEMENT ANALYSIS

By Stanley Burke, M.A.

December 2013: *FBI Law Enforcement Bulletin*

INVESTIGATOR COFFMAN RECENTLY MET WITH A confidential human source (CHS) who claimed to have intelligence regarding criminal activity. He asked the CHS, "So, what's going on?" The CHS responded, "Lots of stuff. I can only stay for a minute, but I have some information you're gonna like—a lot." The source then elaborated.

So, I was at J.J.'s house, and we were talking and eatin' and stuff. We watched the football game. You know, the Leopards have a new quarterback, and he was playing pretty well until he got hurt. They suspect he tore up some ligaments in his knee and won't return until next year. It's too bad he got hurt because they had a good chance of winning the championship this year. They were in first place and all, but now I don't know what's going to happen. Anyway, I believe I kind of see some guns and meth while I'm there. I think it's, sort of like, on his kitchen table, you know, somewhere. Yeah, then we read an ad about a car that was listed in Thursday's newspaper. You know, it was the day they had a picture of that old school house on the front page. The car is located off of Mulberry. It's a cherry Z with ghost flames over a trick red paint job, has a paddle shifter, a 1,000-amp stereo, and has red-tinted rims all the way around. Anyways, he wants me to help him talk to the owner because he thinks I can help him negotiate the price down a bit. Well, I really gotta go. See ya.

The investigator said, "See you next week." After the CHS left, Investigator Coffman reviewed his notes and returned to his office to prepare a contact report, which specifically required him to provide any relevant intelligence provided by the CHS and to include his opinion regarding its reliability. Something about the intelligence made him feel uncomfortable, perhaps, even suspicious. He was not sure how to classify it. While he could not articulate it, Investigator Coffman's "gut" impression can be traced to his CHS's abundance of equivocations, imbalance of critical information, and improper use of present-tense verbs—three useful areas that easily can be analyzed and articulated through the application of basic investigative statement analysis techniques.

WHAT IS STATEMENT ANALYSIS?

Investigative statement analysis involves the examination of the words in a statement to identify indicators of deception.[1] It is a process that provides articulation, depth, and structure to an investigator's instinctual feelings about a statement.

When people intentionally provide deceptive information, they often exhibit a fight-or-flight reaction in response to the increased anxiety level associated with possibly having the deception exposed.[2] As a result, deceptive authors often will attempt to hide behind their own words, phrases, or linguistic construction.[3] To analyze a statement to determine truthfulness, investigators can examine three important areas: equivocations, balance, and verbs.

Then, they can gather assessment data and form an opinion regarding the statement's reliability.

Analyzing Equivocations

Equivocations are words or phrases that allow an author to avoid the risk of commitment. When someone uses equivocations, they actually undermine their own claim, indicating a possible struggle with committing to what has been said.[4] When investigators locate equivocations in a statement, they should view them carefully to determine if the event actually occurred as reported.[5]

As an example, if a person claimed to have been robbed by an unmasked man in broad daylight, the investigator would not expect a statement, such as "I think I was possibly robbed by a man." The victim would be avoiding commitment by using the words *think* and *possibly*. Most robbery victims are certain when they have been robbed, and most can easily identify the sex of the person who robbed them. In this case the investigator would have to question the validity of the victim's statement.

An analysis of the intelligence provided by Investigator Coffman's CHS reveals several meaningful observations. Anyway, I *believe* I *kind of* see some guns and meth while I'm there. *I think* it's, *sort of like,* on his kitchen table, you know, *somewhere.*

The use of equivocations just prior to the introduction of the guns and meth allows the author to avoid specificity regarding exactly what he saw. He never said he saw guns and meth. Rather, he qualified his observation by saying, "I believe I kind of see some" guns and methamphetamine. How does someone "kind of" see such items? Further, he did not commit to a location for the guns and methamphetamine. He stated that they possibly were located on the kitchen table and later said they were somewhere in the house. Moreover, these equivocations are of particular interest inasmuch as the CHS goes into great detail when providing an equivocations-free description of the football game and the vehicle listed in the newspaper.

Examining Statement Balance

Determining statement balance is a simple process. It involves dividing a statement into three sections: an introduction, an event/critical issue, and a conclusion. To begin, the investigator notes when the event phase of a statement starts and ends—the event phase usually starts the moment authors perceive a threat or crime and ends when they indicate that the perceived threat or crime has disappeared.[6]

Once the event is located, the preceding portion of the statement is designated as the introduction, and the following section is identified as the conclusion. Then, the investigator determines what percentage of the statement is dedicated to each portion.[7] A statement should have a balance of approximately 20-60-20. Twenty percent should be dedicated to the introduction, 60 percent to the event, and the remaining 20 percent to the conclusion. The further a statement deviates from the 20-60-20 balance, the more likely it will be deceptive.[8]

Truthful Victim Account

For instance, an assault victim may relay the following:

As I walked out of the restaurant, I noticed a man walking toward me while carrying a broomstick. After we made eye contact, he placed the broomstick over his head, yelled a curse word, and began running in my direction. I immediately ran back into the restaurant and grabbed a big waiter. The man followed me into the restaurant, and when he saw the waiter he yelled more curse words at me, turned, and ran away. I then called 911.

In this example the event started when the victim saw the man place the broomstick over his head—the threat was perceived at that point, not when she first noticed him or made eye contact with him—and it ended when the man ran out of the restaurant. An examination of the victim's statement indicates that the speaker used 80 words to describe the entire incident, 53 to describe the event, 23 to describe the preevent, and 4 to describe the conclusion. In this case the victim's statement has a balance of 28.75–66.25–5, consistent with someone telling the truth.

CHS Statement

An analysis of the intelligence provided to Investigator Coffman has a different result. Concerning the event, the subject revealed little. Anyway, I believe I kind of see some guns and meth while I'm there. I think it's, sort of like, on his kitchen table, you know, somewhere.

In the statement given to Investigator Coffman, the event began the moment his CHS indicated that he perceived criminal activity—the presence of guns and drugs in J.J.'s house—and ended when he ceased talking about the criminal activity. A review of the statement reveals that, overall, it consists of 213 words, of which only 26 (12 percent) are dedicated to the event.

Why is the statement grossly out of balance? The CHS may have minimized the event because it caused him too much stress and tension and because he felt more comfortable talking about the football game and the car for sale, areas he articulated in detail.

Analyzing Verbs

Verbs, of course, describe actions. Typically, when people provide information about past events, they will describe their actions using past-tense verbs, indicating commitment to the past.[9] As an example, if people describe what they ate for breakfast by responding, "I *ate* two eggs and *drank* some orange juice," their answer would contain verbs consistent with actions committed in the past. However, had they answered, "I *eat* two eggs and *drink* some orange juice," their answer would have contained verbs inconsistent with a past action and more consistent with an action presently occurring.

The use of incorrect verb tense possibly indicates deception because deceptive speakers have no past event to refer to. As a result, their mind will create an event, and they will use present-tense verbs to describe it.[10]

An analysis of the intelligence provided to Investigator Coffman reveals the following:

Anyway, I *believe* I kind of *see* some guns and meth while *I'm* there. I think *it's,* sort of like, on his kitchen table, you know, somewhere.

In the statement, the CHS used the proper verb tense when describing his overall visit to J.J.'s house, except when he used past-tense verbs to describe the location of the guns and methamphetamine. Here, the CHS should have said something, such as "Anyway, I believe I kind of *saw* some guns and meth while *I was* there. I'm not positive, but *it was,* sort of like, on his kitchen table, you know, somewhere." This finding presents cause for concern, considering that the CHS used proper verb tense when describing the football game and the vehicle listed in the newspaper. Investigator Coffman now should stop and consider if the portion of the statement containing the improper verb tense did, in fact, occur.

WHAT DO THE RESULTS SHOW?

As a result of examining the statement provided by Investigator Coffman's CHS, it becomes apparent that the intelligence offered has some concerns undermining its validity.

1. The numerous equivocations used to describe the guns and methamphetamine, indicating the author's possible lack of commitment to the intelligence

2. The statement's imbalance, showing that the author may be uncomfortable with his alleged recollection of the event

3. The use of present-tense verbs, revealing that the author may have fictionalized a portion of the intelligence

Did the CHS provide accurate intelligence or not? To be certain, Investigator Coffman must meet again with his CHS and thoroughly review the intelligence to confirm or disprove his results. Until then, Investigator Coffman must refrain from designating his CHS's intelligence as reliable and also consider the subject's motivations for possibly providing unreliable intelligence.

CONCLUSION

Investigative statement analysis is a multistep process that involves much more time and effort than what possibly could be described in this article. However, by simply examining intelligence for equivocations, balance, and verbs, investigators can greatly enhance their opportunity to gain valuable insight and awareness into their CHS's true intention.

Endnotes

[1] Susan Adams, "Statement Analysis: What Do Suspects' Words Really Reveal?" *FBI Law Enforcement Bulletin,* October 1996, 12-20.

[2] Wendell Rudacille, *Identifying Lies in Disguise* (Dubuque, IA: Kendall-Hunt, 1994), 27-33.

[3] Ibid.

[4] Don Rabon, *Investigative Discourse Analysis* (Durham, NC: Carolina Academic Press, 1994), 20.

[5] Susan Adams, "Statement Analysis."

[6] Wendell Rudacille, *Identifying Lies in Disguise,* 134.

[7] Ibid.

[8] Ibid., 135.

[9] Vincent Sandoval, "Interview Clues: Words That Leave an Investigative Trail," *FBI Law Enforcement Bulletin,* January 2008, 1-9.

[10] Ibid.

DISCUSSION QUESTIONS

Assuming the techniques described in this article are valid, what types of situations might they be useful when dealing with human source information related to international security or threat assessment situations?

CRITICAL THINKING EXERCISE

As an investigator, I would never have let the so-called CHS off the hook, and simply walk away—leaving me to undertake some sort of statement analysis in order to determine his reliability. Of course, the author is merely depicting a hypothetical scenario. AS a group, discuss and outline a better plan of action in order to determine the veracity of the informant.

THE ROLE OF EMOTION IN PREDICTING VIOLENCE

By David Matsumoto, Ph.D., Hyi Sung Hwang,
Ph.D., and Mark G. Frank, Ph.D.

January 2012: *FBI Law Enforcement Bulletin*

EMOTION, ONE CRUCIAL ASPECT OF HUMAN BEHAVIOR often overlooked by researchers, operators, and policymakers who often view it as too "soft" for serious consideration or research, serves a crucial purpose in understanding any individual or group behavior. For the individual, emotions are evolved information-processing systems that aid in survival.[1] These transient, fleeting reactions to events can impact a person's welfare and require immediate response.[2] Emotions prime behaviors by initiating unique physiological signatures and mental structures, aid in bonding memories and cognitions, and, most important, serve as a motivator of human behavior.[3]

Group emotions arise when a sufficient proportion of members share similar emotions about their group (the "ingroup") or another group (the "outgroup"), although no definition or consensus in the field exists about what that proportion may be. As in individuals, groups have emotional reactions to events that impact their perceived welfare and survival. Group-level emotions motivate members' behaviors as a whole. Woven into the group's overarching narratives of life, they provide guidelines and bases for making attributions about ingroups and outgroups. They aid in regulating social behavior and preventing social chaos.[4] Thus, a complete understanding of individual or group behavior starts with recognizing the importance of emotion, which is motivation.[5] The authors assert that this is important for recognizing the behavior of individuals and groups in predicting acts of hostility or violence.

Theoretical Framework
Emotions as Discrete Constructs

Many methods exist of understanding and categorizing emotions. For instance, a simple way—popular among laypersons, as well as those in academic psychology— is to classify emotions simply by their valence (positive versus negative) or intensity (strong versus weak); its simplicity merits attention.[6] But, much literature demonstrates convincingly that not all emotions are the same, nor should they be reduced to such simple dimensions as valence or intensity.[7] This framework is known as a *discrete emotions* perspective in which different categories of emotion are qualitatively and uniquely distinct from each other.

For example, considering anger and fear, most law enforcement agencies have heard the phrase "fight or flight" to describe these emotions. Every emotion activates separate areas of the brain and produces different patterns of nonverbal expressions and body reactions (e.g., sweat, surface vasoconstriction vs. dilation), and laypeople do not confuse the subjective sensations associated with them. Someone's expression of fear versus anger has major implications for the person's well-being; inmates who show fear are assaulted, while those who express anger are not. Yet, a valence/intensity model would label both anger and fear similarly as "negative" and "intense."

However, when comparing anger, contempt, and disgust, all, perhaps, negative in terms of valence, important differences among these emotions clearly show that they are not alike, which raises major practical implications. Anger, contempt, and disgust have different physiologies, mental states, and nonverbal expressions, implying different behaviors.[8] Angry people have an increased heart rate, and their blood flows differentially to their arms and hands; this prepares them to fight because anger functions to remove obstacles.[9] However, disgust causes an individual to eliminate or reject contaminated objects. As a primary function, contempt makes someone communicate their evaluations of another's actions vis-à-vis status and hierarchy. Therefore, anger focuses on persons' or groups' actions, while contempt and disgust focus on *who they are*.

Laypersons often do not recognize the important distinctions among emotions. In particular, for several reasons, disgust plays a special role in understanding terrorism and violence. First, studies of emotions in interpersonal conflicts indicate that disgust (and contempt), not anger, contributes to the breakdown of relationships (which also could represent a component of hostile acts between groups).[10] Second, disgust is a basic, primary emotion elicited by the perception of contamination or disease agents.

It is universal, not only in its signal properties but also in terms of its elicitors.[11] Third, disgust is a moral emotion often used to sanction persons' moral beliefs and behaviors.[12] Fourth, anecdotal observations of the videos of terrorists, such as Usama Bin Ladin or Virginia Tech shooter Cho Seung Hui, as well as the speeches and writings of world leaders (e.g., Hitler, Milosevic) who incited wars, revealed an escalation of disgust, as seen in facial expressions, leading up to violent acts. Disgust drives individuals to kill without discretion. For instance, terrorists do not differentiate between men, women, or children; infidels (or vermin) must be eliminated.

Although research on aggression has focused on anger, the authors believe, in today's context of terrorism as a global phenomenon, that disgust must represent a central emotion to study on the group level. There, it represents a shift toward making an assessment of the inherent characteristics of the other group, rather than a temporary judgment about an act committed by that group. Disgust transforms aggression (sometimes constructive) into hostility (usually not) and anger into hatred.

The transformation of anger to contempt and then disgust resembles a conversion of a situational attribution to an act to a dispositional attribution to the person. Consequently, if a person or group does something "bad," anger focuses on the act, but the person or group may or may not be considered bad and, in fact, may be rehabilitated somehow in the future. Evaluations resulting in contempt and disgust, however, indicate that the person or group is inherently bad and there is no chance for rehabilitation; thus, the logical recourse is to eliminate them. Elimination can occur in various ways, from extreme forms of violence to shunning, avoiding, or simply dissociating them.

Intergroup Emotions
While the scientific study of emotion traditionally has focused on the individual, in recent years, it increasingly has centered on group emotions. Most studies have examined the types of emotions felt by members of groups toward outgroups. For instance, studies suggest that intergroup anxiety toward outgroups may occur because of potential

embarrassment about not knowing what to do with the outgroup's members, apprehension about negative behavioral consequences, fear of disapproving evaluations, past negative intergroup relations, minimal previous contact with the outgroup, large status differences between the ingroup and outgroup, or higher ratios of outgroup members compared with ingroup members (more of "them" than "us").[13] Studies on the Stereotype Content Model suggest that group members have different emotions toward outgroups based on the dimensions of perceived warmth and competence.[14] The Intergroup Emotions Theory suggests that ingroup members feel anger toward an outgroup it is in conflict with when the ingroup view is that of the majority; this anger will lead to confronting, opposing, or attacking the outgroup.[15]

Studies also have examined the emotions attributed to ingroup and outgroup members. For example, the Infrahumanization Theory suggests that ingroup favoritism and outgroup derogation leads to the attribution of more human characteristics, including emotions, toward the ingroup.[16]

Thus, ingroups more likely will attribute the more human emotions of compassion, shame, serenity, bitterness, or contempt to ingroup members. At the same time, ingroups attribute more basic (or primary) emotions, such as surprise, anger, pleasure, fear, attraction, or disgust, to outgroups.

Researchers consider these emotions shared between humans and primates.[17]Thus, the dehumanization of outgroups involves the attribution of emotions associated with animals to the outgroups, and intergroup emotions keep such attitudes about outgroups connected. Without their emotional bases, these attitudes would have little meaning or practical consequence. But, intergroup relations are complex and potentially deadly, especially among ideologically based groups, precisely because outgroup cognitions are associated with strong emotions.

Emotions and Escalation to Violence
Cultures of Emotion-Based Hatred

Because emotions function primarily to motivate behavior on both the individual and group levels, not only are they instrumental in creating and maintaining intergroup attitudes and relations but changes in those emotions over time may become associated with different intergroup behaviors. In the authors' view, violence and hostility directly result from the planned inculcation and careful, methodical nurturing of hatred in terrorist groups. This theoretical framework is based on a view of discrete emotions, most notably those related to morality.[18]

Although such emotions as shame and guilt have received considerable attention as moral emotions in the past, more recent work has focused on anger, contempt, and disgust and their relationship to autonomy, community, and divinity.[19] Specifically, some experts have proposed that anger, contempt, and disgust often result from violations of community, autonomy, and divinity, respectively known as the CAD Triad Hypothesis.[20]

Another expert has proposed a triarchic theory of hatred based on anger, contempt, disgust, and fear.[21] He proposes that hatred is based on 1) a negation of intimacy (originating from disgust); 2) passion (resulting from anger and fear); 3) and decision-commitment deriving from the devaluation and diminution of others (based on contempt). According to his model, different kinds of hatred can exist based on different combinations of these three components. Because there are three components, they can yield seven different combinations of hatred:

cold, cool, hot, simmering, boiling, seething, and burning.

An interesting aspect of his theory is that hatred is propagated via stories or narratives.[22] Stories serve an important and interesting purpose, bringing to life the various components of hatred in a concise, easy-to-understand and easy-to-communicate method. They provide group leaders with a platform by which shared emotions can be developed, fostered, maintained, or extinguished; in turn, group members communicate those stories to others. Many different types of hate stories achieve this purpose.[23]

- Strangers
- Impure others (versus pure ingroup members)
- Controllers (versus controlled)
- Faceless foes (versus individuated ingroup members)
- Enemies of God (versus servants of God)
- Morally bankrupt persons (versus morally sound individuals)
- Death (versus life)
- Barbarians (versus civilized ingroup members)
- Greedy enemies (versus financially responsible ingroup members)
- Criminals (versus innocent parties)
- Torturers (versus victims)
- Murderers (versus victims)
- Seducer-rapists (versus victims)
- Animal pests (versus humans)
- Power-crazed individuals (versus mentally balanced persons)
- Subtle infiltrators (versus infiltrated)
- Comic characters (versus sensible ingroup members)
- Thwarter-destroyers of destiny (versus seekers of destiny)

Stories also serve the important function of providing members a way to communicate attitudes, values, beliefs, and opinions across generations, a central component of culture that refers to a shared meaning and information system transmitted across generations.[24]Unique cultures characterize terrorist groups. Cultural systems provide guidelines for normative behavior, the basis for the nature and function of attributions, communication systems, and intergroup relations. Sacred values and beliefs also characterize terrorist organizations but, then again, also many ideologically-based organizations.[25]

Research on terrorists and other ideologically based groups suggests comparability to each other in their social-psychological dynamics.[26] A culture of disdain permeated throughout the group facilitates hatred of others, and future generations are similarly enculturated. Emotionally laden narratives color the perception of all new data; group members accept at face value information that confirms the narrative and dismiss details that disconfirm the narrative through accusations of bias, conspiracies, or even flat-out logical fallacies.[27] Once established, narratives become self-perpetuating.

Emotions Leading to Violence
Building on these theoretical frameworks, the authors propose that emotions transform over time, often via stories, to inculcate cultures with hatred and violence. Specifically, this emotional transformation follows three phases.

Phase 1: Outrage Based on Anger
This involves the group identifying events that obstruct goals or stem from perceived injustice. It also may involve the group identifying threats to its well-being, physical safety, or way of life. These interpretations

and attributions lead to or are fueled by feelings of anger toward the outgroup.

Phase 2: Moral Superiority Based on Contempt Groups begin to reinterpret anger-eliciting situations and events identified in Phase 1 and take the high road. That is, they reappraise the events from a position of moral superiority and identify links between similar behaviors or events, no matter how tenuous, thus, making the attribution that the outgroup is morally inferior. These reappraisals and attributions lead to or are fueled by the emotion of contempt.

Phase 3: Elimination Based on Disgust A further reappraisal of events and situations leads to the conclusion that distance is necessary (the mild form of elimination) between the ingroup and outgroup or that the outgroup needs to be removed altogether (the extreme form). These ideas are promulgated by the emotion of disgust.

This perspective helps to understand that groups can hate, but that not all hatred leads to violence or hostility. Hatred based primarily on anger or contempt likely will not be associated with violence or hostility, but hatred that involves disgust—the emotion of repulsion and elimination—likely will be. Groups can be angry or contemptuous but, when also disgusted, they may become dangerous. Further, interestingly, many definitions of hatred involve concepts of intense aversion related to the emotions of disgust or intense animosity, which has its roots in animals and also relates to disgust.

How do these appraisals and reappraisals occur and group emotions get created or transformed? Powerful leaders set the tone for groups to interpret or reinterpret events in certain ways that then lead to group emotions. Leaders do this by creating stories based on their appraisals or reappraisals of critical events and situations and by communicating the emotions associated with their reappraised stories to their followers and subordinates. The communication occurs through specific types of emotion-laden words, metaphors, images, and analogies, as well as nonverbally through their faces, voices, gestures, and body language.

That is, emotions are not communicated directly to groups (e.g., we perceived an obstacle, so we must be angry). Instead, emotions are communicated indirectly via the associations made to groups with emotion-laden words, metaphors, analogies, and nonverbal behaviors. Through the careful use of language and nonverbal behaviors, leaders can motivate, escalate, or defuse situations and incite action—or not—through emotion.

Empirical Evidence
Recently, the authors conducted an initial test of these ideas by examining the emotions expressed by world leaders and heads of ideologically motivated groups in archived speeches about outgroups the leaders despised. There never had been a formal analysis of the emotional content of such statements, and archives served as a rich source of information that allowed the authors to test the hypothesis that verbal expressions of anger, contempt, and disgust toward outgroups over time lead to violence and hostility against that group.

The authors anchored these speeches to an identified act of aggression and selected for analysis those speeches available at five specified points in time (3, 6, 12, 18, and 24 months) prior to the acts of aggression. They also included for comparison a small group of acts and speeches of ideologically motivated groups that focused on hated outgroups but did not result in violence.

The authors analyzed the speeches for their emotional content and tested the differences in that content, separating the ones from groups that committed an act of aggression from those that did not, which they labeled acts of resistance. The authors hypothesized that acts of aggression would be characterized by an increase in anger, contempt, and disgust as speeches toward the outgroups neared the event, whereas acts of resistance would follow where there was no increase in these emotions.

As predicted, acts of aggression were associated with increases in anger, contempt, and disgust in the time periods immediately preceding the act of aggression. Interestingly, acts of resistance followed *decreases* in these emotions during this same time period. There were no differences in any other emotions for acts of aggression or resistance. These findings were not affected by the time when the events occurred as separate analyses of only events within the last 50 years produced the same results.

These findings demonstrated how an analysis of specific emotions of anger, contempt, and disgust—not just any negative emotion—proves especially meaningful in terms of understanding how group emotions contribute to aggression or hostility. As mentioned, anger is about what an individual or a group did; however, contempt and disgust focus on who people or groups are. The combination of contempt and disgust, along with anger, allows groups and individuals to make emotional dispositions about the moral character of others. When people and groups feel contempt and disgust toward others, they are evaluating the target of their contempt and disgust as inherently bad or contaminated. No chance for rehabilitation exists; the only logical recourse is elimination. Anger focuses on actions, but not necessarily the underlying morality of the act or the individuals or groups performing it. Martin Luther King, Jr., Mahatma Gandhi, and the Dalai Lama all have been angry and, perhaps, even contemptuous, but they did not become disgusted with their outgroups.

Although the findings from the authors' study demonstrated that the emotions expressed in the language used by leaders of ideologically motivated groups determined groups' violence, emotions expressed in the words may constitute only part of the overall emotional message delivered. Nonverbal behaviors, such as facial expressions and tones of voice, that accompany the emotionally laden language probably amplify the overall emotional messages delivered. Therefore, quite possibly, when emotionally laden language is imbedded within a rich repertoire of nonverbal behaviors that also portray emotions, the overall emotional message to the listeners may hold substantially more power than simply reading the words. The authors currently are researching this possibility.

Facial Expressions of Emotion and Aggression
Signs of Imminent Aggression

Another line of the authors' research program has attempted to identify the nonverbal signals of imminent aggression. This work holds the view of emotions as evolved, rapid information-processing systems that enable humans to adapt to changes in their environment with minimal conscious intervention.[28] When elicited, emotions recruit a host of physiological, cognitive, and expressive behaviors organized and coordinated with each other.[29] Facial expressions constitute part of this coordinated response package. Charles Darwin claimed, in his principle of serviceable habits, that facial expressions are the residual actions of more complete, whole-body responses that prepare individuals for action by priming the body to act.[30] Thus, people express anger when furrowing their brow and tightening their lips with teeth displayed because these actions form part of an attack response. Individuals show disgust with an open mouth, nose wrinkle, and tongue protrusion as part of a vomiting response. Recent research has suggested that different facial expressions (e.g., those showing fear and disgust) facilitate the acquisition or rejection of sensory information.[31]

This important theoretical perspective suggests a link between specific facial expressions of emotion and subsequent behavior. Although disgust may energize the narrative to produce violence at a distal level, anger energizes the physical action of assault at the proximal level.

Recently, the authors examined the possibility that variants of the facial expression of anger represent a reliable association with acts of immediate, subsequent violent behavior. Logically, signs of anger may arise prior to acts of aggression or assault if anger primes the body to aggress, and facial expressions are part of the anger-response package. Given that assassinations, shootings, and physical violence often occur in a matter of seconds, the existence of such facial signs is a distinct possibility and has important practical ramifications.

In the authors' studies, a single Caucasian male—a professional actor—demonstrated an array of faces for law enforcement officers (LEOs) in five countries. Each expression depicted a variant of the full-face, prototypic version of anger found in stimulus sets, such as the Pictures of Facial Affect or the Japanese and Caucasian Facial Expressions of Emotion stimulus sets.[32] That is, all expressions included at least some of the muscles identified by the Facial Action Coding System (FACS) involved in the full-face prototype; the expressions differed in the amount and intensity of those muscles and in the presence or absence of *zygomatic major* (the smiling muscle).[33]

The expressions were generated by first asking the actor to produce the face seen in previous videos involving assaults, attacks, and assassination attempts. Additional expressions then were portrayed when the actor demonstrated as many different kinds of anger as he knew. This resulted in a preliminary selection of 16 expressions. Pilot testing with a separate group of American LEOs indicated that some of the expressions almost never were selected in the procedures; 4 expressions were, thus, dropped, resulting in a final stimulus set of 12 expressions, which the authors placed in a random array and numbered.

LEOs in each of the countries selected a face from the 12 that they saw moments before either a premeditated physical assault or an assault due to a momentary loss of impulse control. Prior to this task, the LEOs were asked if they ever were involved in such attacks, if they remembered the face of the attacker, and if they could recall the face if they saw it again. The LEOs identified 2 faces—1 for premeditated assaults and 1 for loss of impulse control—at high agreement rates. Moreover, LEOs in different countries, two of which were non-English speaking, identified the same faces.

University students shown the same set of faces and engaged in the same experimental procedures did not select the same faces at the previous chance rates, suggesting that the authors' findings did not result from a process of elimination among the 12 provided. More recently, the authors replicated the findings with

LEOs and university students using a different array of faces, ensuring that the initial findings were not limited to a single expresser.

Potential Research Possibilities

The authors hope to expand the notion of violence from the spontaneous and planned to include the special category of suicide bombers, particularly those who believe they have divine dispensation to conduct their attack. The authors have no data concerning the facial signs of this type of imminent aggression and have no reason to believe that the face of the suicide bomber is the same as that of the person carrying out a premeditated attack or who loses control and attacks. They would like to study additional video footage prior to a violent event for signs of impending attack through both facial expressions and bodily movements, such as gait or tension.

Moreover, additional questions can follow on this line of research. For example, the authors have developed tools to help train individuals to identify the two types of dangerous faces identified by LEOs in their studies; as of this date, however, they have no data concerning its efficacy either as a training tool or in the field. Such data are a must. The authors have developed the necessary experimental protocols and plan to conduct their research within a relatively short period of time.

Implications

The findings to date have significant potential implications for national defense and security, intelligence, and law enforcement operations. For example, the elucidation of the role of emotion in leading to acts of aggression by members of ideologically motivated groups suggests the existence of signs that can serve as markers of escalation toward hostility. This, combined with the creation of sensor technologies that can recognize those markers, either through the analysis of the emotional content of verbal statements, nonverbal behavior, or the emotional profiles of groups, leads to the interesting potential for these markers to predict hostile acts before enacted, allowing for evasive or preemptive action that may save lives.

Technologies that analyze the verbal content of speeches can identify emotions associated with this escalation, allowing for the production of automated detectors of aggression potential based on ramp-ups of disgust across time. The same potential exists for automated detectors of aggression ramp-ups based on video analyses of faces or voices.

These technological advances all are predicated on the establishment of empirically validated signs of aggression escalation based on emotion, which have been found preliminarily but require further validation. The identification of facial signs of premeditated assault leads to the interesting possibility that automated expression-recognition technologies can be developed to scan crowds for such faces to identify individuals of interest; this capability surely would be useful for those in the protective services. And, the identification of the face displaying a loss of impulse control is important for anyone who interacts with individuals who may explode to violence at any time.

Conclusion
Emotions are essential to understanding individual and group behavior as they serve to motivate. Gaining an understanding of this behavior can help predict acts of hostility and violence.

In today's world, agencies need as many tools as possible to carry out their mission of protecting the public. The authors offer their findings in this regard.

Knowing what signs to look for is important for anyone potentially in harm's way.

Endnotes

1 L. Cosmides and J. Tooby, "Evolutionary Psychology and the Emotions," in *Handbook of Emotions*, ed. M. Lewis and J.M. Haviland-Jones (New York, NY: Guilford Press, 2000), 91-115; and C. Darwin, *The Expression of Emotion in Man and Animals* (New York, NY: Oxford University Press, 1998).

2 P. Ekman, *Emotions Revealed* (New York, NY: Times Books, 2003); and R. Lazarus, Emotion and Adaptation (New York, NY: Oxford University Press, 1991).

3 R.W. Levenson, "The Intrapersonal Functions of Emotion," *Cognition and Emotion* 13, no. 5 (1999): 481-504; R.W. Levenson, "Autonomic Specificity and Emotion," in *Handbook of Affective Sciences*, ed. R.J Davidson, K. Scherer, and H.H. Goldsmith (New York, NY: Oxford University Press, 2003), 212-214; G.H. Bower, "Mood and Memory," *American Psychologist* 36, no. 2 (1981): 129-148; J.P. Forgas and H.G. Bower, "Mood Effects on Person-Perception Judgments," *Journal of Personality and Social Psychology* 53, no. 1 (1987): 53-60; S.S. Tomkins, *Affect, Imagery, and Consciousness (Vol 1: The Positive Effects)* (New York, NY: Springer, 1962); and S.S. Tomkins, *Affect, Imagery, and Consciousness (Vol 2: The Positive Effects)* (New York, NY: Springer, 1963).

4 D. Matsumoto, S.H. Yoo, S. Nakagawa, J. Alexandre, J. Altarriba, M. Arriola, A.M. Anguas-Wong, and L.M. Bauer, "Culture, Emotion, Regulation, and Adjustment," *Journal of Personality and Social Psychology* 94, no. 6 (2008): 925-937.

5 Tomkins, *Affect, Imagery, and Consciousness (Volumes 1 and 2)*.

6 J.A. Russell and L. Feldman Barrett, "Core Affect, Prototypical Emotional Episodes, and Other Things Called Emotion: Dissecting the Elephant," *Journal of Personality and Social Psychology* 76, no. 5 (1999): 805-819.

7 P. Ekman, "Basic Emotions," in *The Handbook of Cognition and Emotion*, ed. T. Dalgleish and T. Power (Sussex, UK: John Wiley and Sons, 1999), 45-60; C.E. Izard, "Basic Emotions, Natural Kinds, Emotion Schemas, and a New Paradigm, "*Perspectives on Psychological Science* 2, no. 3 (2007): 260-280; and J. Panksepp,

"Neurologizing the Psychology of Effects: How Appraisal-Based Constructivism and Basic Emotion Theory Can Coexist," *Perspectives on Psychological Science* 2, no. 3 (2007): 281-296.

[8] Ekman, "Basic Emotions," 1999, 45-60.

[9] Levenson, "Autonomic Specificity and Emotion," 2003, 212-214.

[10] J. M. Gottman and R.W. Levenson, "A Two-Factor Model for Predicting When a Couple Will Divorce: Exploratory Analyses Using 14-Year Longitudinal Data," *Family Process* 41, no. 1 (2002): 83-96; and J. M. Gottman, R.W. Levenson, and E. Woodin, "Facial Expressions During Marital Conflict," *Journal of Family Communication* 1 (2001): 37-57.

[11] P. Ekman, "Facial Expression and Emotion," *American Psychologist* 48, no. 4 (1993): 384-392; P. Rozin, J. Haidt, and C.R. McCauley, "Disgust: The Body and Soul Emotion," in *Handbook of Cognition and Emotion*, ed. T. Dalgleish and M.J. Power (Sussex, UK: John Wiley and Sons, 1999), 429-445; and P. Rozin, L. Lowery, S. Imada, and J. Haidt, "The CAD Triad Hypothesis: A Mapping Between Three Moral Emotions (Contempt, Anger, Disgust) and Three Moral Codes (Community, Autonomy, Divinity)," *Journal of Personality and Social Psychology* 75, no. 4 (1999): 574-585.

[12] H.A. Chapman, D.A. Kim, J.M. Susskind, and A.K. Anderson, "In Bad Taste: Evidence for the Oral Origins of Moral Disgust," *Science* 323 (2009): 1222-1226.

[13] P.M. Niedenthal, S. Krauth-Gruber, and F. Ric, *Psychology of Emotion: Interpersonal, Experiential, and Cognitive Approaches* (New York, NY: Psychology Press, 2006); and W.G. Stephan and C.W. Stephan, "Intergroup Anxiety," *Journal of Social Issues* 41 (1985): 157-175.

[14] A.J.C. Cuddy, S.T. Fiske, and P. Glick, "The BIAS Map: Behaviors from Intergroup Affect and Stereotypes," *Journal of Personality and Social Psychology* 92, no. 4 (2007): 631-648.

[15] D.M. Mackie, T. Devos, and E.R. Smith, "Intergroup Emotions: Explaining Offensive Action Tendencies in an Intergroup Context," *Journal of Personality and Social Psychology* 79, no. 4 (2000): 602-616.

[16] B.P. Cortes, S. Demoulin, R.T. Rodriguez, A.P. Rodrigues, and J.P. Leyens, "Infrahumanization or Familiarity?

Attribution of Uniquely Human Emotions to the Self, the Ingroup, and the Outgroup," *Personality and Social Psychology Bulletin* 31, no. 2 (2005): 243-253; S. Demoulin, J.P. Leyens, M.P. Paladino, R. Rodriguez Torres, A. Rodriguez Perez, and J.F. Dovidio, "Dimensions of 'Uniquely' and 'Nonuniquely' Human Emotions," *Cognition and Emotion* 18 (2004): 71-96; and R. Rodriguez Torres, J.P. Leyens, B. Cortez, A. Perez Rodriguez, V. Betancour Rodriguez, M.N. Quiles del Castillo, and S. Demoulin, "The Lay Distinction Between Primary and Secondary Emotions: A Spontaneous Categorization?" *International Journal of Psychology* 40, no. 2 (2005): 100-107.

[17] J.E. LeDoux and E.A. Phelps, "Emotional Networks in the Brain," in *Handbook of Emotions*, ed. M. Lewis, J.M. Haviland-Jones, and L. Feldman Barrett (New York, NY: Guilford Press, 2008), 159-179.

[18] Ekman, "Basic Emotions," 1999, 45-60; P. Rozin and A.E. Fallon, "A Perspective on Disgust," *Psychological Review* 94, no. 1 (1987): 23-41; Rozin, Haidt, and McCauley, "Disgust: The Body and Soul Emotion," 1999, 429-445; and J. Tangney and K.W. Fischer, ed., Self-Conscious Emotions: *The Psychology of Shame, Guilt, Embarrassment, and Pride* (New York, NY: Guilford Press, 1995).

[19] R.A. Shweder and J. Haidt, "The Cultural Psychology of the Emotions: Ancient and New," in *The Handbook of Emotions*, ed. M. Lewis and J.M. Haviland (New York, NY: Guilford Press, 2000), 397-414; Tangney and Fischer, *Self-Conscious Emotions*, 1995; and Rozin et al, "The CAD Triad Hypothesis," 1999, 574-585.

[20] Rozin, Haidt, and McCauley, "Disgust: The Body and Soul Emotion," 1999, 429-445.

[21] R.J. Sternberg, "A Duplex Theory of Hate: Development and Application to Terrorism, Massacres, and Genocide," *Review of General Psychology* 7, no. 3 (2003): 299-328.

[22] Sternberg, "A Duplex Theory of Hate," 2003, 299-328.

[23] Sternberg, "A Duplex Theory of Hate," 2003, 299-328.

[24] D. Matsumoto and L. Juang, *Culture and Psychology* (Belmont, CA: Wadsworth, 2007).

[25] S. Atran and R. Axelrod, "Sacred Barriers to Conflict Resolution," *Science* 317 (2007): 1039-1040; S. Atran and R. Axelrod, "Sacred Barriers to Conflict Resolution," Science

317 (2007): 1039-1040; and J. Ginges, S. Atran, D. Medin, and K. Shikaki, "Sacred Bounds on Rational Resolution of Violent Political Conflict," *Proceedings from the National Academy of Sciences* 104 (2007): 7357-7360.

[26] A. Stahelski, "Terrorists are Made, Not Born: Creating Terrorists Using Social Psychological Conditioning," *Cultic Studies Review* 4, no. 1 (2005).

[27] R.E. Nisbett and L. Ross, *Human Inference: Strategies and Shortcomings of Social Judgment*(Englewood Cliffs, NJ: Prentice Hall, 1980).

[28] Ekman, "Basic Emotions," 1999, 45-60; Lazarus, *Emotion and Adaptation*, 1991; and J. Tooby and L. Cosmides, "The Evolutionary Psychology of the Emotions and Their Relationship to Internal Regulatory Variables," in *Handbook of Emotions*, ed. M. Lewis, J.M. Haviland-Jones, and L. Feldman Barrett (New York, NY: Guilford Press, 2008): 114-137.

[29] Levenson, "The Intrapersonal Functions of Emotion," 1999, 481-504.

[30] C. Darwin, *The Expression of Emotion in Man and Animals*, 1998.

[31] J.M. Susskind, D.H. Lee, A. Cusi, R. Feiman, W. Grabski, and A.K. Anderson, "Expressing Fear Enhances Sensory Acquisition," *Nature Neuroscience* 11 (2008): 843-850.

[32] P. Ekman and W.V. Friesen, *Pictures of Facial Effect* (Palo Alto, CA: Consulting Psychologists Press, 1976); and D. Matsumoto and P. Ekman, "Japanese and Caucasian Facial Expressions of Emotion and Neutral Faces (JACFEE and JACNeuF); available from *http://humintell.com*.

[33] P. Ekman and W.V. Friesen, *Facial Action Coding System: Investigator's Guide* (Palo Alto, CA: Consulting Psychologists Press, 1978).

DISCUSSION QUESTIONS

CRITICAL THINKING EXERCISE

LASER POINTER ATTACKS TAKING OFF:
POSE SERIOUS THREAT TO AVIATION SECURITY

October 2012: *FBI Law Enforcement Bulletin*

IF YOU'VE EVER THOUGHT ABOUT POINTING A HAND-HELD laser at an aircraft of any kind, think again. It's highly dangerous and a federal crime.

The number of laser attacks in the U.S. is on the rise. Incidents are projected to reach 3,700 this year— compared to just 283 in 2005. That's a rise of more than 1,100 percent. And that doesn't include the thousands of attacks that go unreported every year.

George Johnson, a supervisory federal air marshal who is a liaison officer with the FBI, says the number of attacks is almost reaching an "epidemic level."

In recent years, technology has improved the performance and power of handheld lasers; the Internet has also made these gadgets cheaper and easier to purchase.

These incidents are dangerous to pilots in the cockpit, passengers aboard the plane, and people on the ground. Captain Robert Hamilton of the Air Line Pilots Association, International was landing a plane when he was struck by a laser light. "I had temporary blindness. My eyes were burning. It caused disorientation, and it was distracting," he says.

To combat the threat, the FBI last year established a Laser Strike Working Group National Initiative, which includes law enforcement partners and private entity stakeholders. The idea came from the FBI's Sacramento Division, which created the first Laser Strike Working Group in 2008 to reduce incidents in the area. It worked—the number of attacks against commercial aircraft arriving and departing from the Sacramento International Airport decreased 75 percent.

Those who aim a laser pointer at an aircraft can be prosecuted under two federal statutes. A law put into effect this year makes pointing a laser at an aircraft a crime punishable by up to five years in prison and a fine of up to $11,000 per violation. Under a law already on the books, those who interfere with the operation of an aircraft can receive up to 20 years in prison and be fined $250,000.

"Use a laser pointer for what it's made for. Aiming a laser pointer at an aircraft is dangerous and reckless. Just don't do it," says Johnson.

To report a laser attack, dial 911. You can also e-mail the Federal Aviation Administration at laserreports@FAA.gov or contact your nearest FBI field office.

DISCUSSION QUESTIONS

From a behavioral analysis standpoint, why do you think individuals engage in laser attack practices such as those described in this article? Support your answer based upon facts, theoretical frameworks, or sound hypothesis.

CRITICAL THINKING EXERCISE

The authors make a claim that the Laser Strike Working Group reduced attacks by 75% in 2008. Are there any data that exist, which may serve to support such a claim? If so, what did the Working Group actually do to account for such decrease?

CROWD MANAGEMENT
ADOPTING A NEW PARADIGM
By Mike Masterson

August 2012: *FBI Law Enforcement Bulletin*

MANAGING CROWDS IS ONE OF THE MOST IMPORTANT tasks police perform. Whether or not members of the public agree with this practice, they often judge how well law enforcement officers achieve this—if it is done fairly and effectively. Of course, officers should treat everyone with respect and courtesy without regard to race, gender, national origin, political beliefs, religious practice, sexual orientation, or economic status. Although perhaps daunting, the primary function of police is relational, whether they respond to a domestic dispute, investigate a crime, enforce a traffic regulation, or handle a crowd. Once officers understand this, they will find it easier to determine what to do and how to do it.[1]

LESSONS LEARNED
Studied by law enforcement for at least 40 years, crowd control is important due to the dangers posed by unruly gatherings. To this end, it proves fair to ask whether police leaders do all they can to share lessons learned and incorporate best practices into crowd management philosophy, training, and tactics.

As a young police officer in Madison, Wisconsin, in the 1970s, the author experienced the Vietnam War's aftermath at home and the eruptions of student unrest.

A state capital and home to a major university, Madison at times is a hotbed for protests. From antiapartheid demonstrations and dismantling of shantytowns on capitol property to an annual alcohol-laden Halloween festival, the author, along with fellow officers, monitored and managed partiers and protesters for over four decades. With groups ranging from 6 church members to 250,000 people celebrating in a city park, Madison police successfully balanced rights to assembly and free speech with citizen and officer safety.

The author benefited from those lessons on crowd management when becoming chief of the Boise, Idaho, Police Department in 2005. The city subsequently hosted the National Governors' Conference and the 2009 Special Olympics World Winter Games. Boise police officers manage a wide variety of protests, parades, and demonstrations on issues, such as immigration, human rights, and most recently, a death penalty execution and Occupy Boise.

A police chief's involvement and direction prove critical to officers' ability to successfully manage emotional, potentially volatile crowds. The message received from top-level management greatly influences the behavior and mind-set of frontline officers. Shaping these attitudes begins with a solid understanding that police work involves building relationships with members of the public whom officers are sworn to serve and protect.

BRITISH INFLUENCE

The International Association of Chiefs of Police (IACP) and the Police Executive Research Forum (PERF) have an increasing amount of information available on best practices in crowd management. PERF's recent publication *Managing Major Events: Best Practices from the Field* contains insight offered by law enforcement leaders from the United States and Canada on what has worked for them.[2]

This report includes the Vancouver, British Columbia, Police Department's new policy on tolerance and restraint when dealing with crowds. Police leadership in Vancouver recognized the success of British crowd control policies, sent their senior executives overseas to study the model, and brought back trainers to assist officers with implementing this new style of crowd control during the 2010 Winter Olympics.

With British input, Vancouver police developed a meet-and-greet strategy. Instead of using riot police in menacing outfits, police officers in standard uniforms engaged the crowd. They shook hands, asked people how they were doing, and told them that officers were there to keep them safe. This created a psychological bond with the group that paid dividends. It becomes more difficult for people to fight the police after being friendly with individual officers.[3]

British research on policing crowds confirms the strategic need for proactive relationship building by police. In the 1980s, a professor at the University of St. Andrews in Scotland published early findings on how law enforcement tactics shape crowd identity and behavior.[4]

Later, a doctor at the University of Liverpool published research on hooliganism—rowdy, violent, or destructive behavior—at British soccer games. Named after fans of a soccer club involved in two riots with South Wales Police in 2001 and 2002, the Cardiff Approach is based on two leading theories of crime reduction—the Elaborated Social Identity Model

(ESIM), the leading scientific theory of crowd psychology, and the Procedural Justice Theory (PSJ).

The ESIM maintains that crowd violence escalates if people think police officers treat them unfairly. PSJ proposes that group members comply with the law when they perceive that officers act with justice and legitimacy.[5] When a crowd becomes unruly and individuals perceive unfair treatment by law enforcement officers, violence can escalate, and a riot can erupt. Recent research finds support for both perspectives and concludes that when police officers act with legitimacy, disorder becomes less likely because citizens will trust and support law enforcement efforts and behave appropriately.[6]

THE MADISON METHOD

Modern research supports a philosophy of public order policing from the 1970s referred to as The Madison Method of Handling People in Crowds and Demonstrations.[7] This approach begins with defining the mission and safeguarding the fundamental rights of people to gather and speak out legally. The philosophy should reflect the agency's core values in viewing citizens as customers. This focus is not situational; it cannot be turned on and off depending on the crisis.

Law enforcement agencies facilitate and protect the public's right to free speech and assembly. When officers realize they are at a protest to ensure these rights, they direct their responses accordingly, from planning to implementing the plan. Officers must have a well-defined mission that encourages the peaceful gathering of people and uses planning, open communication, negotiation, and leadership to accomplish this goal.

Los Angeles Police Department (LAPD) commanders achieved success in planning and communicating their agency's mission during an Occupy Los Angeles gathering. Throughout the event, officers' objective was to facilitate the peaceful removal of all people and their belongings from the city hall park area. Participants received a reasonable amount of time to leave, after which officers issued a dispersal order. Anyone refusing to exit the park faced arrest.[8]

Officers should begin with constructive engagement, dialogue, and a soft approach. British law enforcement agencies call this the "softly-softly approach." Law enforcement personnel mingle and relate to the crowd using low-key procedures based on participants' behavior, rather than their reputation or officers' preconceived notions of their intent.

Police and demonstration organizers should coordinate prior to an event. This re-enforces law enforcement's role as facilitator, rather than confronter. Maintaining dialogue throughout the event helps minimize conflict. Of course, dialogue involves two-way conversation— sometimes this means listening to unpopular opinions and suggestions. There is only one crowd; however, individuals comprise that mass. If the event is peaceful, officers should remain approachable to, for instance, give the location of the nearest ATM, provide the phone number for a taxi, or supply directions to a parking lot.

Public Order Policing Model

An effective public order policing model has several components. The foundation begins with scientific theory and evidence based on researched and tested techniques. Effective contemporary crowd control methods used by American, Canadian, and British agencies support these techniques. Police procedures strongly influence law enforcement training, thus, affecting officers' responses.

Police Response

Police Training

Police Policy, Knowledge, and Philosophy → The Madison Method — 1975
→ The Cardiff Approach — 2001
→ The Vancouver Model — 2010

Science-Based, Event-Tested Theoretical Understanding of Crowds

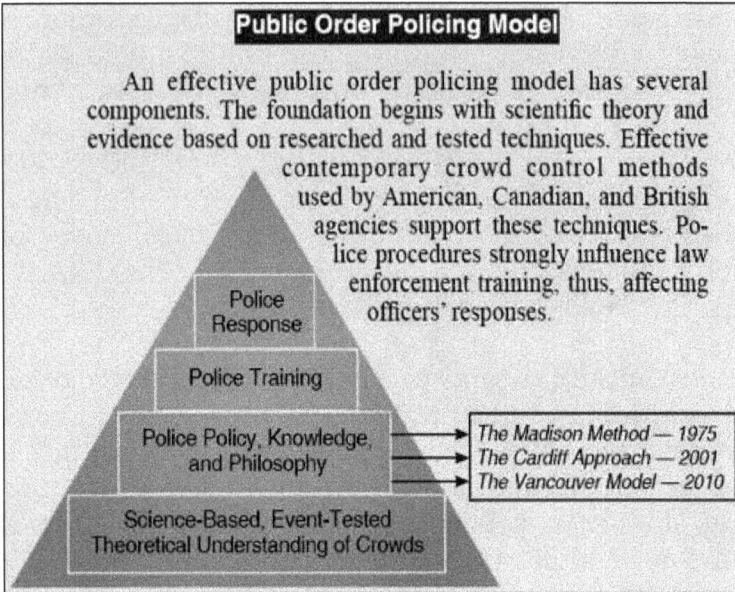

Officers must avoid donning their hard gear as a first step. They should remember lessons learned from the 1960s civil rights movement and Vietnam War protests. Police should not rely solely on their equipment and tools.[9] Experience shows that when used as a primary tactical option in public order policing, dialogue is invaluable. Law enforcement officers must defuse confrontations to ensure strong ties with the community. If they fail, rather than stronger community goodwill, the effect will be less civility and the erosion of constitutional rights.[10]

NEGOTIATION AND EDUCATION

Officers must negotiate, educate, and maintain continual dialogue with organizers and crowd members. Police personnel initially must state that they defend the public's right to demonstrate, but cannot allow the crowd to hurt others or destroy property. Whether officers support the crowd's position or if the group holds an unpopular view, law enforcement agencies must remain neutral and prevent physical injuries or property destruction. If arrests become necessary, police officers must respect individuals and avert harm to anyone in custody. Officers must convey that they expect cooperation in return.

Recently, an elected leader in Boise recognized the need for officers to address crowd management questions. It became apparent that some demonstrators misinterpreted law enforcement agencies' approach. While police engaged in reasonable, steady conversation, the public sometimes saw this as uncaring, which indicated the importance of educating demonstrators early. In Vancouver, officers quickly relayed to Winter Olympics fans the strategy to keep everyone safe.

PROTECTION AND PROFESSIONALISM

Protecting officers who work with a crowd is important. The Stockholm, Sweden, Police Department uses highly visible and identifiable "dialogue police," while British law enforcement agencies use "communication police." The Boise Police Department, maintains a tactical unit with full protective equipment on standby in an out-of-sight location near the demonstration. The unit serves as an emergency response to protect officers and the public from harm. Its mission is to safeguard people first and property second. Deploying the emergency response team is a last alternative when soft crowd control tactics prove ineffective.

Law enforcement agencies can show leadership in preparation and training for events by using specially qualified police officers. The best officers to use in crowd control situations are those specifically selected and trained who have the personality to use a soft approach under difficult circumstances. Self-control proves essential.

Not all police officers can manage multitudes

effectively. Crowd control offers a rare opportunity for agencies to cultivate a positive public image. When officers operate as a team, the public observes confidence and professionalism far above any uniformed presence.

ACCOUNTABILITY AND VISIBILITY

While restraining from the employment of force is important, its use may become necessary at large gatherings, especially those born out of passion. Officers working at large events must realize that someone watches and records all arrests. Police officers with up-to-date training in making team arrests ensure efficient apprehensions.

Avoiding the use of outside agencies can be wise. Officers from other locations may differ in philosophy, training, or ability to work together during a conspicuous event. External resources could lack soft crowd management experience or community knowledge. It proves important to local agency leaders that officers take personal responsibility for crowd management in their city.

Occasionally, outside help proves necessary. A recent event in Boise required the participation of five large agencies consisting of state, county, and city forces. The effort was well-planned and coordinated. Success came from all stakeholders' early planning and clear understanding of the mission.

Avoiding anonymity and promoting accountability are essential. By ensuring police officers assigned to crowd control are identifiable, with names and badge numbers clearly visible, agencies prevent their officers from becoming anonymous agents. Obscurity or depersonalization of officers encourages negative crowd behavior and leads to unaccountable actions.

Agencies should videotape events. Segments recorded by participants, bystanders, and media are useful; however, when departments record their own documentation, they ensure its value for case review, accountability, and context. The University of California, Berkeley, Police Department has such a practice. Normally, it videotapes all demonstrations or crowd situations to ensure complete records of the event. During periods in which violations, police actions, or other significant activities occur, the agency employs at least two video cameras.[11] To safeguard the First Amendment and privacy rights of those participating in the event, agencies should adopt a policy governing retention and destruction of these tapes.

During high-profile or large demonstrations, police command officers must remain on the scene, visible, interactive, and willing to take charge. This provides an excellent opportunity to assess the mood of the crowd and reinforce the agency's outlook and crowd management tactics.

COMMUNICATION AND PREPARATION

With 24-hour news, cell phone cameras, Facebook, Twitter, and hundreds of other social media connections, it becomes important to prevent potentially dangerous rumors from appearing as facts. Because of erroneous witness statements and other misleading or false information, justifiable use of force has triggered riots.

Law enforcement agencies play a major role in responsibly reporting accurate information quickly and continually for the benefit of officers, the public, and the media. Although officers are not responsible for inaccurate reporting, developing a proactive, engaged media plan is important. Social media serves as an excellent way to directly communicate department messages and obtain information on events.

Law enforcement agencies must have a plan to de-escalate conflict situations. If an arrest becomes necessary, the individual taken into custody should be one who threatens the peace of the event. Sometimes, officers disperse a crowd to preserve harmony and prevent injuries and property damage. Police officers with specialized skills and equipment do this best. Law enforcement agencies must prepare for circumstances that suddenly can turn a crowd confrontational.

At any large demonstration, law enforcement officers primarily serve as peacekeepers facilitating lawful intentions and expressions. Participants perceive the legitimacy of police actions based on how officers interact with the crowd throughout an event. Communicating expectations, negotiating continually, and emphasizing the goal of safety are vital. Officers should not confuse the actions of a few with those of the group. Law enforcement personnel must remain firm, fair, and professional.

CONCLUSION
Commonplace instant, mass, and social media provide an opportunity to highlight and improve the public's view of law enforcement legitimacy. Using communication and best practices in crowd management, officers reinforce their position as peacekeepers. Police, the most visible form of government, must continue to ensure that the First Amendment rights of the public they serve are protected and guaranteed.

ENDNOTES
[1] D. Couper, *Arrested Development: One Man's Lifelong Mission to Improve Our Nation's Police* (Madison, WI: Dog Ear Publishing, 2012).

2 D. LePard, *Managing Major Events: Best Practices from the Field* (Washington, DC: Police Executive Research Forum, 2011).

3 LePard, *Managing Major Events.*

4 S.D. Reicher, "The St. Paul's Riot: An Explanation of the Limits of Crowd Action in Terms of a Social Identity Model," *European Journal of Social Psychology* 14 (1984): 1-21; and S.D. Reicher, "Crowd Behavior as Social Action," in J.C. Turner, M.A. Hogg, P.J. Oakes, S.D. Reicher, and M.S. Wetherell, *Rediscovering the Social Group: A Self Categorisation Theory* (Oxford, UK: Basil Blackwell, 1987).

5 C. Stott, "Study Identifies Best Approach to Policing Football Matches," *University of Liverpool, UK, University News*, October 20, 2011, *https://news.liv.ac.uk/2011/10/20study-identifies-best-approach-to-policing-football-matches/?utm_source=University+News&utm_medium=email&utm_term=26-10—11&utm_campaign=fortnightly+update* (accessed April 19, 2012).

6 C. Stott, "Crowd Psychology and Public Order Policing: An Overview of Scientific Theory and Evidence" (presented to the HMIC Policing of Public Protest Review Team, University of Liverpool, UK, School of Psychology, September 2009).

7 The Madison Method of handling people in crowds and demonstrations was created by Chief David Couper, Madison, WI, Police Department, and staff in the 1970s.

8 U.S. Department of Homeland Security, Federal Emergency Management Agency, Incident Management System, Incident Command System (ICS) Form 202, National Commander's Intent, Occupy Los Angeles, November 29-30, 2011.

9 L. Reiter, "Occupy and Beyond: Practical Steps for Reasonable Police Crowd Control," Legal and Liability Risk Management Institute (LLRMI), *http://www.llrmi.com/articles/legal_update/2011_crowd_control.shtml* (accessed December 13, 2011).

10 A. Baker, "When the Police Go Military," *New York Times*, December 3, 2011,*http://www.nytimes.com/2011/12/04/sunday-review/have-american-police-become-militarized.html?_r=1&sq*

=When%20the%20Police%20Go%20Military&st=cse (accesse
d June 19, 2012).
[11] University of California, Berkeley, Police Department,
"Crowd Management
Policy,"http://administration.berkeley.edu/prb.PRBCrowdPo
licy.pdf (accessed December 12, 2011).

DISCUSSION QUESTIONS

1. Given the recommendations in this article, do you believe that most modern police departments would take such an approach?

2. Do you think there would be any major differences in the approaches to crowd control between urban or suburban police departments, or rural sheriffs and/or state police forces? Explain your position.

CRITICAL THINKING EXERCISE

This article is based upon the demonstrators' legal right to assemble as guaranteed under the First Amendment of the Constitution. There is no question in my mind that most—if not all—of the recommendations of the author are spot on.

For this exercise, and working as a group, assume that the assembly is indeed unlawful. This could mean the demonstrators did not obtain a proper permit, are trespassing on private property, or another factor other than a lawful demonstration that happened to turn unlawful due to acts of violence or disorderly conduct.

Based upon concepts discussed in this article, develop a plan for handling the initial contact with an unlawful group, but where there is no violence or threats of violence at that moment.

Agroterrorism
Threats to America's
Economy and Food Supply

By Dean Olson, M.A.

February 2012: *FBI Law Enforcement Bulletin*

THE UNITED STATES ENJOYS A SAFE, PLENTIFUL, AND inexpensive food supply. Americans spend only 11 percent of their income on food compared with the global average of 20 to 30 percent.[1] The nation's agricultural abundance helps drive its economic prosperity. As many as 1 of 6 jobs are linked to agriculture, a trillion-dollar industry. Agriculture-related products comprise nearly 10 percent of all U.S. exports, amounting to nearly $68 billion in 2006.[2]

Terrorists consider America's agriculture and food production tempting targets. They have noticed that its food supply is among the most vulnerable and least protected of all potential targets of attack. When American and allied forces overran al Qaeda sanctuaries in the caves of eastern Afghanistan in 2002, among the thousands of documents they discovered were U.S. agricultural documents and al Qaeda training manuals targeting agriculture.

A subset of bioterrorism, *agroterrorism* is defined as "the deliberate introduction of an animal or plant disease for the purpose of generating fear, causing economic losses, or undermining social stability."[3] It represents a tactic to attack the economic stability of the United States. Killing livestock and plants or contaminating food can help terrorists cause economic crises in the agriculture and food industries. Secondary goals include social unrest and loss of confidence in government.

Serious Concern
Agroterrorism is not new. The Assyrians poisoned enemy wells with rye ergot during the 6th century B.C. During World War I, German agents in the United States infected horses and cattle in transit across the Atlantic to France. In 1994, in The Dalles, Oregon, a religious cult intentionally contaminated 10 restaurant salad bars with salmonella, sickening more than 750 people in an attempt to influence the outcome of a local election. Since 1912, 12 documented cases have involved the substate use of pathogenic agents to infect livestock or contaminate food.[4]

The agroterrorism threat emanates from four categories of perpetrators. The foremost threat is posed by transnational groups, like al Qaeda—widely believed to present the most probable threat of inflicting economic harm on the United States.

The second group is comprised of economic opportunists tempted to manipulate markets. They understand that a foot and mouth disease (FMD) outbreak, for example, would have a dramatic impact on markets. By introducing the virus, they could exploit the markets for personal economic gain.

The third category includes domestic terrorists who may view the introduction of FMD as a blow against the federal government. As an outlier of this category, the unbalanced individual or disgruntled employee may perpetrate an attack for a variety of idiosyncratic or narcissistic motivations.

Finally, militant animal rights or environmental activists pose a threat because they consider immoral the use of animals for food. Groups, such as the Animal Liberation Front and its sister organization, the Earth Liberation Front, could view an attack on the animal food industry a positive event.[5]

Threat Environment

Because it lacks the drama and spectacle of more common terrorist violence, such as bombings and murders, agroterrorism has remained a secondary consideration, and no documented attacks in the homeland have occurred since 9/11. Several recent factors may have made agroterrorism a more attractive tactic.

First, the threat environment has changed dramatically. America has had recent successes against al Qaeda's leadership. These victories have forced the group to morph in both structure and tactics. The increasingly dangerous environment it now must operate in has prevented it from mounting catastrophic terrorist attacks on the scale of 9/11. Now, al Qaeda places its emphasis on smaller, independent attacks following a "death by a thousand cuts" strategy to exhaust, overwhelm, and distract U.S. Department of Homeland Security forces. The group seeks to flood America's already information overloaded intelligence systems with myriad threats and "background noise."[6] Agroterrorism also may serve as a way to magnify the social upheaval caused by smaller, independent attacks, like bombings.

Second, Usama Bin Ladin consistently had argued that attacking the U.S. economy represented the best way to destroy America's ability to project military power abroad. Underpinning this view is al Qaeda's historical narrative that jihad against the Soviets following the invasion of Afghanistan led not only to the defeat of the Red Army but, ultimately, to the demise of the U.S.S.R.[7] As divorced from reality as this view seems, economic harm remains one of the pillars of al Qaeda's terror strategy against the United States. In a video broadcast before the 2004 U.S. presidential elections, Usama Bin Ladin bragged that his organization "...bled Russia for 10 years until it went bankrupt and was forced to withdraw in defeat.... We are continuing in the same policy to make America bleed profusely to the point of bankruptcy...."

He boasted that the 9/11 attacks had cost al Qaeda $500,000 while inflicting a staggering $500 billion in economic losses to America.[8] According to Bin Ladin, "every dollar of al Qaeda defeated a million dollars [of America]...besides the loss of a huge number of jobs." Analysts believe that al Qaeda's evolving tactics increasingly will "focus on targets that will yield the most economic damage."[9]

Terrorist leaders realize that America's strength stems largely from its economic vitality. They pursue an overarching strategy that all attacks should focus on weakening America's economic strength, especially through protracted guerilla warfare. In their view, as the United States loses its standing in the Middle East, groups, like al Qaeda, can gain ground and remove from power regimes they view as corrupt and illegitimate.[10]

Terrorists know that a successful agroterrorism incident threatens America's economic welfare and its standing as a leading exporter of agricultural products to the world. A significant disruption in agricultural exports caused by such an attack would have ripple effects in the United States' and global economies. This economic disruption would occur on three levels.

The first involves direct losses due to containment measures, such as stop-movement orders (SMOs) or quarantines of suspected stock. Additional costs would arise from the culling and destruction of disease-ridden livestock.[11] Second, indirect multiplier effects, such as compensation to farmers for destruction of agricultural commodities and losses suffered by directly and indirectly related industries, would arise.[12] And, third, international costs would result from protective trade embargoes. Less measurable consequences would include the undermining of confidence in and support of government, creation of social panic, and threat to public health on the national and global levels.

Given its ease of execution and low cost to high benefit ratio, agroterrorism fits the evolving strategy of al Qaeda that focuses on inexpensive but highly disruptive attacks in lieu of monumental ones. Agroterrorism could exacerbate the social upheaval caused by random bombings. The ability to employ cheap and unsophisticated means to undermine America's economic base, combined with the added payoff to potentially overwhelm its counterterrorism resources, makes livestock- and food-related attacks increasingly attractive.[13]

Foot and Mouth Disease
Attacks directed against the cattle, swine, or poultry industries or via the food chain pose the most serious danger for latent, ongoing effects and general socioeconomic and political disruption. Experts agree that FMD presents the most ominous threat.[14] Eradicated in the United States in 1929, FMD remains endemic in South America, Africa, and Asia.[15] An especially contagious virus 20 times more infectious than smallpox, FMD causes painful blisters on the tongues, hooves, and teats of cloven-hoofed animals, including cattle, hogs, sheep, goats, and deer,

rendering them unable to walk, give milk, eat, or drink. Although people generally cannot contract the disease, they can carry the virus in their lungs for up to 48 hours and transmit it to animals. The animal-to-animal airborne transmission range is 50 miles.[16] An infected animal can shred the virus in large quantities from its upper respiratory tract via drooling, coughing, and discharging mucus. Extremely stable, FMD can survive in straw or clothing for 1 month and spread up to 100 kilometers via the wind. Because herds exist as highly crowded populations bred and reared in extremely close proximity to one another, a significant risk exists that such pathogenic agents as FMD will spread well beyond the locus of a specific outbreak before health officials become aware of a problem. An FMD outbreak could spread to as many as 25 states in as little as 5 days simply through the regulated movement of animals from farm to market.[17]

From a tactical perspective, an FMD attack holds appeal for several reasons. First, unlike biological warfare directed against humans, no issue of weaponization exists. In an FMD attack, the animals themselves serve as the primary medium for pathogenic transmission, and countries as close as those in South America offer a ready source of the virus. As one analyst described it, the virus "can be spread by simply wiping the mucus from an infected animal on a handkerchief and then transferring the virus to healthy animals by wiping their noses...by stopping on a highway in rural America and releasing the virus among curious livestock an outbreak could be initiated."[18]

Second, FMD is nonzoonotic, presenting no risk of accidental human infection. There exists no need for elaborate personal protective equipment or an advanced understanding of animal disease science. In a biowarfare attack targeting people, the deadly pathogen poses a threat to the perpetrators, as well as their intended victims. Preparing the pathogen so that terrorists can handle it safely yet disseminate it effectively to intended victims can prove difficult. For instance, the Aum Shinrikyo sarin gas attacks on the Tokyo subway in 1994 largely failed to kill the number of people intended due to the crude method of dissemination.

Third, terrorists could introduce and subsequently disperse the virus throughout the American food production system through multiple carriers, including animals carrying and introducing it into susceptible herds; animals exposed to contraband materials, such as contaminated food, hay, feedstuffs, hides, or biologics; people wearing clothing or using equipment, including tractors and trucks, to transmit the virus to uninfected animals; and contaminated facilities, such as feed yards, sale barns, and trucks that commonly hold or transport susceptible animals.[19]

The same factors that yield inexpensive and plentiful food by promoting maximum production efficiency also make American agricultural systems inherently vulnerable. The highly concentrated and intensive nature of livestock production encourages the rapid spread of contagious pathogens.[20] Most dairies house at least 1,500 cows, with the largest facilities containing 10,000. Animals often are born on breeding farms and then transported to another state for slaughtering and processing. Otherwise isolated and widely dispersed farms often share equipment, vehicles, and veterinary instruments. Feedlots and auctions routinely intermingle animals from a wide geographic area. On average, a pound of meat travels 1,000 miles before it reaches the consumer's table.[21]

The introduction of FMD would require the mass slaughter and disposal of infected animals. An outbreak could halt the domestic and international sale of meat and meat products for years. In this regard, in 2001, FMD in the United Kingdom affected 9,000 farms and required the destruction of more than 4,000,000 animals. Researchers believe that a similar outbreak in the United States would cost taxpayers up to $60 billion.[22] An FMD attack could result in massive herd culling, the need to destroy processed goods, and extensive decontamination efforts of production and livestock-containment facilities. Most Americans have not witnessed the intense media coverage of high-volume culling operations involving the destruction and disposal of tens of thousands of animals. Large-scale eradication and disposal of livestock likely would be especially controversial as it affects farmers and ranchers and offends the sensibilities of animal rights activists and environmental organizations.

Food Production and Distribution
If terrorists strive for human deaths, the food production and distribution chain offers a low-tech but effective mechanism for disseminating toxins and bacteria, such as botulism, E. coli, and salmonella. Developments in the farm-to-table continuum greatly have increased the number of entry points for these agents. Many food processing and packing plants employ large, unscreened seasonal workforces. They commonly operate uneven standards of internal quality and inadequate biosurveillance control to detect adulteration.[23]These vulnerabilities, combined with the lack of security at many processing and packing plants, contribute to the ease of perpetrating a food-borne attack.

Beyond the economic and political impact, low-tech bioterrorist assaults against the food chain have the potential to create social panic as people lose confidence in the safety of the food supply. A large-scale attack potentially could undermine the public's confidence in its government. Because most processed food travels to distribution centers within a matter of hours, a single case of chemical or biological adulteration could have significant latent ongoing effects, particularly if the source of the contamination is not immediately apparent and there are acute ailments or deaths.[24] Supermarkets in major American cities stock only a 7-day supply of food; therefore, any significant and continuing disruption in supply quickly will lead to severe shortages.

Experts believe that fruit- and vegetable-packing plants are among the most vulnerable venues for food-borne attacks. Many represent small-scale manufacturers that specialize in ready-to-eat meats or aggregated foodstuffs. They do not practice uniform biosecurity methods, and they do not use heat, an effective front-end barrier against pathogens, in food processing. Also, because they deal in already-prepared produce that does not require cooking—a good back-end defense against microbial introduction—they provide a viable portal to introduce pathogens.

Law Enforcement Preparedness
Farms, ranches, and feedlots in America are dispersed, open, and generally unprotected. The majority of state and local law enforcement agencies face financial and strategic challenges when responding to agroterrorism, yet the laws of many states treat agroterrorism as a crime investigation, giving local law enforcement agencies primary responsibility.

An outbreak of FMD would exhaust law enforcement resources quickly. After recognition of the disease by state agriculture authorities, subsequent steps in the emergency response involve containment and eradication, often involving multiple herds and a large quarantine area that may encompass multiple counties. State agriculture authorities working with the U.S. Department of Agriculture's Animal and Plant Health Inspection Service have responsibility and authority for animal disease.[25] Specially trained animal health officials make decisions on disease control, such as livestock quarantine and the timing and method of livestock depopulation—culling, destroying, and disposing of diseased animals from infected herds by burning or burial.

Following strict biosecurity measures can prevent the spread of disease. Local and state law enforcement would play a pivotal role in this effort by adhering to three primary responsibilities.

First, police officials would enforce quarantine orders given by state agriculture authorities. This involves isolating and containing infected stock to prevent the spread of disease. A quarantine area would comprise a 6-mile radius, approximately 113 square miles, surrounding the point of origin; numerous roadblocks would prevent vehicles, equipment, or persons from entering or leaving without detailed decontamination measures and authorization.[26] Inside the quarantine area, officials would establish an "exposed zone" in which all cloven-hoofed animals would be destroyed. For effectiveness, quarantine of infected premises and SMOs would have to remain in effect for a minimum of 30 days.[27]

The second responsibility occurs in conjunction with quarantine. Officers would enforce SMOs issued by the state governor to prevent the spread of the disease.[28] Initial biosecurity efforts could require placement of all animals under an SMO. Law enforcement may be empowered to restrict human and animal movement in and out of the quarantine zone. This authority would include all animals in transit within a wide geographic area until the investigation clarified the extent of the infection and determined which animals can move safely. Although FMD affects only cloven-hoofed animals, humans, horses, and other animals may carry the virus.

Enforcing an SMO would require care and shelter for animals in transit that must be temporarily unloaded and housed at local sites providing feed and water.[29] During the SMO, law enforcement would interview drivers to determine points of origin and destinations of animals. Research indicates that officers would stop and evaluate an average of nearly 50 vehicles per hour in the first day of an SMO.

Third, the criminal investigation of the outbreak further would tax already strained law enforcement resources. The investigation would focus on identifying the source of the virus and the mechanism used to infect susceptible animals. The danger of additional infections by the perpetrators would make the criminal investigation time sensitive.

Many law enforcement agencies lack the sufficient resources and procedures to simultaneously cope with quarantines, SMOs, and criminal investigations while also staffing widely dispersed checkpoints around the clock for the duration of the emergency. When combined with the need also to deliver routine law enforcement services, most agencies would struggle to meet these demands, especially during the protracted nature of an FMD outbreak.

Conclusion
Agriculture may not represent terrorists' first choice of targets because it lacks the shock factor of more traditional attacks; however, it comprises the largest single sector in the U.S. economy, making agroterrorism a viable primary aspiration. Such terrorist groups as al Qaeda have made economic and trade disruption key goals. They believe that by imposing economic hardship on America, its citizens

will tire of the struggle and force their elected leaders to withdraw from commitments abroad.

Every level of the food chain, including farms, feedlots, chemical storage facilities, meatpacking plants, and distribution operations, remains vulnerable to agroterrorism. Because terrorists rely on a lack of preparedness, law enforcement agencies should develop a plan to prevent agroterrorism and minimize the results of an attack. Officers must investigate from an agroterrorism perspective thefts of livestock; a criminal organization may steal animals with the intent of infecting them and placing them back into the population. Thefts of vaccines, medicines, and livestock-related equipment should be of concern and carefully investigated. It also is vital that law enforcement officials forward reports of such incidents to their states' intelligence-fusion centers, threat-integration centers, or law enforcement intelligence units or networks.

Endnotes
[1] U.S. Census Bureau, *Statistical Abstract of the United States: 2004-2005* (Washington, DC, 2004), 234.
[2] U.S. Department of Agriculture, Economic Research Service, *Foreign Agricultural Trade of the United States (FATUS): Monthly Summary December 2006*; retrieved from *http://www.ers.usda.gov/ Data/FATUS/MonthlySummary.htm* (accessed May 25, 2011).
[3] Jim Monke, Congressional Research Service Report for Congress, *Agroterrorism: Threat and Preparedness*; retrieved from *http://www.fas.org/ sgp/crs/terror/RL32521.pdf* (accessed May 25, 2011).
[4] Terry Knowles, James Lane, Gary Bayens, Nevil Speer, Jerry Jaax, David Carter, and Andra Bannister,*Defining Law Enforcement's Role in Protecting American Agriculture from Agroterrorism*; retrieved from*http://www.ncjrs.gov/ pdffiles1/nij/grants/212280.pdf* (accessed May 25, 2011).
[5] Knowles et al., *Defining Law Enforcement's Role in Protecting American Agriculture from Agroterrorism*,22.

6 Bruce Hoffman, "Al Qaeda Has a New Strategy. Obama Needs One, Too"; retrieved from *http://www.washingtonpost.com/ wp-dyn/content/article/2010/01/08/AR2010010803555.html? sid=ST2010031703003* (accessed on May 25, 2011).
7 Bruce Hoffman and Gabriel Weimann, "Econo-Jihad"; retrieved from *http://nationalinterest.org/ article/econo-jihad-3120* (accessed on May 25, 2011); and UPI.com, "Jihadists Turning to Economic Terrorism"; retrieved from *http://www.upi.com/ Top_News/US/2010/03/02/Jihadists-turning-to-economic-terrorism/ UPI-97581267548984/* (accessed on May 25, 2011).
8 Daveed Gartenstein-Ross, "Al Qaeda's Oil Weapon"; retrieved from *http://www.weeklystandard.com/ Content/Public/Articles/ 000/000/006/163cchwz.asp* (accessed on May 25, 2011).
9 Gabriel Weimann, "Jihadists Turning to Economic Terrorism"; retrieved from *http://www.upi.com/ Top_News/US/2010/03/02/Jihadists-turning-to-economic-terrorism/ UPI-97581267548984/* (accessed on May 25, 2011).
10 Weimann, "Jihadists Turning to Economic Terrorism."
11 Peter Chalk, "Hitting America's Soft Underbelly: The Potential Threat of Deliberate Biological Attacks Against the U.S. Agricultural and Food Industry"; retrieved from *http://www.rand.org/ pubs/monographs/2004/RAND_MG135.pdf* (accessed on May 25, 2011).
12 Peter Chalk, "The U.S. Agricultural System: A Target for al Qaeda?" *Terrorism Monitor* 3, no. 5 (2005).
13 Chalk, "The U.S. Agricultural System: A Target for al Qaeda?"
14 Knowles et al., *Defining Law Enforcement's Role in Protecting American Agriculture from Agroterrorism,*3.
15 U.S. Department of Agriculture, Animal and Health Inspection Service, *APHIS Factsheet: Foot-and-Mouth Disease*; retrieved from *http://www.aphis.usda.gov/ publications/ animal_health/content/ printable_version/fs_foot_mouth_disease07.pdf* (accessed on May 25, 2011).
16 Glenn R. Schmitt, "Agroterrorism—Why We're Not Ready: A Look at the Role of Law Enforcement"; retrieved

from *http://www.nij.gov/ journals/257/agroterrorism.html* (accessed on May 25, 2011).

[17] Chalk, "The U.S. Agricultural System: A Target for al Qaeda?"

[18] John Grote, Jr., "Agroterrorism: Preparedness and Response Challenges for the Departments of Defense and the Army"; retrieved from *http://www.aepi.army.mil/ publications/sustainability/docs/ agroterror-prep-resp.pdf* (accessed on May 25, 2011).

[19] Knowles et al., *Defining Law Enforcement's Role in Protecting American Agriculture from Agroterrorism,*98.

[20] Dean T. Olson, original research for the Center for Homeland Defense and Security (Naval Postgraduate School, Monterey, CA, 2004).

[21] Chalk, "Hitting America's Soft Underbelly: The Potential Threat of Deliberate Biological Attacks Against the U.S. Agricultural and Food Industry," 8.

[22] U.S. Department of Agriculture, *Economic Impact of a Foreign Animal Disease (FAD) Outbreak Across the United States* (Washington, DC, 2004).

[23] Chalk, "The U.S. Agricultural System: A Target for al Qaeda?"

[24] Chalk, "The U.S. Agricultural System: A Target for al Qaeda?"

[25] Janice P. Mogan, "Overview of a Foreign Animal Disease Response"; retrieved from *http://www.agr.state.ne.us/ division/bai/overview_foreign_animal_disease_response.pdf* (accessed on May 25, 2011).

[26] Knowles et al., *Defining Law Enforcement's Role in Protecting American Agriculture from Agroterrorism,*4.

[27] Knowles et al., *Defining Law Enforcement's Role in Protecting American Agriculture from Agroterrorism,*92.

[28] U.S. Department of Agriculture, *Economic Impact of a Foreign Animal Disease (FAD) Outbreak Across the United States.*

[29] Knowles et al., *Defining Law Enforcement's Role in Protecting American Agriculture from Agroterrorism,*92.

DISCUSSION QUESTIONS

Do you believe that U.S. authorities at the federal, state, and local levels are prepared to prevent or respond to any degree of agroterrorism?

CRITICAL THINKING EXERCISE

Conduct some preliminary research to see if there have actually been incidences of any form of agroterrorism in the United States or whether credible intelligence has been developed that would indicate the real possibility of such an eventuality.

Economic Espionage: Competing For Trade By Stealing Industrial Secrets

By Christopher Munsey

November 2013: *FBI Law Enforcement Bulletin*

IN SEPTEMBER 2012 FBI AGENTS IN KANSAS CITY, Missouri, arrested two Chinese nationals, Huang Ji Li and Qi Xiao Guang, after they paid $25,000 in cash for stolen trade secrets pertaining to an American company's manufacture of cellular-glass insulation, or foam glass. Huang trespassed onto the company's flagship plant in Sedalia, Missouri, 3 months prior and asked suspiciously detailed questions about the facility's manufacturing process for the insulation. It also is believed he approached an employee at the company's corporate headquarters in Pittsburgh, Pennsylvania, just days before seeking to build a foam-glass factory in China.

The company is the world's leader in developing and manufacturing cellular-glass insulation; its Missouri plant produces about 90 percent of stock. The trademarked, lightweight, fireproof, and mold-resistant product is useful as insulation in buildings, industrial piping systems, and liquefied-natural-gas storage-tank bases. China represents a strong market for this type of insulation.

In November 2010 sparks ignited flammable foam insulation during the renovation of a high-rise apartment building in Shanghai, resulting in an inferno that killed at least 58 people and injured scores more. Reacting to public anger over the death toll, municipal governments began requiring fireproof insulation in new construction. Cellular-glass insulation is an ideal solution, particularly for Chinese developers who need to build up, not out, in space-constrained towns and cities.

Weeks after the trespass, managers at the company's plant received a call from the Sedalia daily newspaper about an advertisement submitted online from an e-mail traceable to China.

Technical talent wanted to explore together Asian market. You are equipped with more than 10 years experience on foam glass...? You are able to lead a project to build up a foam glass factory with continuous research on new formulas. You are willing to adventure in Asia for couple of years? We prepared battle field for you.

Concerned by the message, company leadership contacted local police and the FBI's Kansas City office. The Sedalia Police Department investigated the trespassing, taking statements from plant employees who witnessed two men walking around the factory property. Police also obtained credit card information from the local hotel where the trespassers stayed during their visit. Their findings helped FBI investigators confirm Huang as a suspect.

A judge sentenced Huang to 18 months in prison and a $250,000 fine in January 2013 and Qi, Huang's interpreter, to time served, a $20,000 fine, and deportation. During sentencing, company officials estimated the value of the targeted trade secrets at $272 million. Investigators believe that Huang, whose family owned two factories making plastic toys in China, had the capital needed to build a cellular-glass factory, with a site lined up, construction plans in place, and enough knowledge of chemical manufacturing to put the stolen secrets to use.

TARGETS FOR THEFT

Although the Missouri case ended in arrests and convictions, officials say U.S.-based businesses, academic institutions, cleared defense contractors, and government agencies increasingly are targeted for economic espionage and theft of trade secrets by foreign competitors, often with state sponsorship and backing. In the last fiscal year alone, economic espionage and theft of trade secrets cost the American economy more than $19 billion.

Over the past 4 fiscal years, the number of arrests related to economic espionage and theft of trade secrets overseen by the FBI's Economic Espionage Unit has almost doubled, indictments have more than tripled, and convictions have increased sixfold. Halfway through fiscal year 2013, the number of open investigations is running more than 30 percent above the total from 4 years ago.

Theft of trade secrets, often called industrial espionage, occurs when someone knowingly steals or misappropriates a trade secret to the economic benefit of anyone other than the owner. Similarly, economic espionage occurs when a trade secret is stolen for the benefit of a foreign government, foreign instrumentality, or foreign agent. Proving the foreign nexus in court is difficult, and cases that start out as economic espionage often end up prosecuted as theft of trade secrets. Both are covered by the Economic

Espionage Act of 1996, Title 18, Sections 1831 and 1832, U.S. Code.

Experts say economic espionage and theft of trade secrets increasingly are linked to the insider threat and the growing threat of cyber espionage.[1] The insider threat is created by employees with legitimate access to information. The employee who poses an insider threat may be stealing information for personal gain or may be serving as a spy to benefit another organization or country. Foreign competitors conduct economic espionage by aggressively targeting and recruiting insiders; conducting economic intelligence through bribery, cyber intrusions, theft, and dumpster diving (in search of intellectual property or discarded prototypes); and establishing joint ventures with U.S. companies.

China often is cited as particularly active in the theft of trade secrets. According to a report submitted to Congress by the U.S.-China Economic and Security Review Commission in November 2012, China "depends on industrial espionage, forced technology transfers, and piracy and counterfeiting of foreign technology as part of a system of innovation mercantilism."[2] By obtaining what it needs illegally, China avoids the expense and difficulty of basic research and unique product development, the report concluded.

THREAT RESPONSE
Enhanced Strategies for Law Enforcement
Officials across the U.S. government are pursuing a comprehensive strategy to counter economic espionage as part of a larger campaign against intellectual property theft. In furtherance of this initiative, the U.S. Department of Justice formed a task force on intellectual property in February 2010. The task force works with the Office of the Intellectual Property

Enforcement Coordinator (IPEC), located in the Executive Office of the President. In February 2013 IPEC released a strategy on mitigating the theft of U.S. trade secrets. The strategy calls for focusing diplomatic efforts to protect trade secrets overseas, promoting voluntary best practices by private industry to protect trade secrets, enhancing domestic law enforcement operations, improving domestic legislation, and boosting public awareness and stakeholder outreach.

The FBI also is reaching out to government agencies and private companies to help counter the insider threat and cyber intrusions through its network of strategic partnership coordinators (SPCs) located in each of the bureau's 56 field offices. SPCs currently maintain more than 15,000 contacts nationwide, consisting of local businesses, academic institutions, and cleared defense contractors.

They help educate employees on how to protect trade secrets and encourage employers to require nondisclosure agreements from employees and contractors. To help protect trade secrets, companies need to mark sensitive material as secret or proprietary information, limit access to protected material, and monitor who accesses it. FBI investigators should be called in as soon as an insider threat is suspected and be given a chance to conduct a logical investigation.

Increased Penalties for Offenders
Congress responded last year to the growing threat of economic espionage by approving tougher penalties for those convicted of the crime. Formerly, an individual responsible for economic espionage faced a maximum fine of $500,000; Congress passed legislation boosting this maximum to $5 million. Additionally, organizations responsible for committing economic espionage now face penalties greater than the previous

maximum of $10 million, up to three times the value of stolen trade secrets.

Congress also directed the U.S. Sentencing Commission to examine the sentencing guidelines for economic espionage and theft of trade secrets. Following public hearings, the commission approved a two-level increase in sentencing guidelines earlier this year. If a trade secret is taken out of the country or if a defendant knows the trade secret will benefit a foreign government, possible prison time for the offender will increase from between 15 to 21 months to 21 to 27 months. The guidelines will go into effect in November 2013 unless amended by Congress.

CONCLUSION

The threat of economic espionage and theft of trade secrets to U.S.-based companies is persistent and requires constant vigilance. Even after Huang was arrested, pled guilty, and was sentenced, investigators believed the company's trade secrets still were at risk for targeting by would-be competitors. Officials hope the possibility of larger fines and longer sentences will prompt defendants to strike plea agreements with prosecutors and cooperate more with investigators to explain the methods and participants in economic espionage conspiracies.

Endnotes

[1] U.S. Sentencing Commission, "Public Hearing on Proposed Amendments to the Federal Sentencing Guidelines, March 13, 2013," under "Panel I: Economic Espionage: Part I (Executive Branch Panel)," *http://www.ussc.gov/Legislative_and_Public_Affairs/Public_Hearings_and_Meetings/20130313/Transcript.pdf*(accessed July 22, 2013).

[2] U.S.-China Economic and Security Review Commission, *2012 Report to Congress,* 112th Cong., 2d sess. (Washington, DC: Government Printing Office, 2012): 421.

DISCUSSION QUESTIONS

One of the key components of the U.S. Air Force Office of Special Investigations (OSI), from which I retired, is to protect critical technologies and information and to engage foreign adversaries and threats offensively.* Indeed, these assets involve most of our nation's top secret capabilities. How do you think the behavioral analysis techniques you have learned thus far may have some application to enhancing investigations and/or prosecutions for economic espionage in regard to Department of Defense research, technologies, and methods?

* http://www.osi.andrews.af.mil/main/welcome.asp

CRITICAL THINKING EXERCISE

The article discusses—in general terms—some of the enhanced strategies to combat economic espionage. Examples given include focusing diplomatic efforts to protect trade secrets overseas, promoting voluntary best practices by private industry to protect trade secrets, enhancing domestic law enforcement operations, improving domestic legislation, and boosting public awareness and stakeholder outreach.

What does this all mean? For example, what do you think some of the "best practices" in relation to preventing economic espionage are?

FBI COUNTERINTELLIGENCE DIVISION'S BEHAVIORAL ANALYSIS PROGRAM: A UNIQUE INVESTIGATIVE RESOURCE

By Robin K. Dreeke

July 9, 2013: *FBI Law Enforcement Bulletin*

THE FBI'S NUMEROUS INVESTIGATIVE PROGRAMS PRESENT many challenges, buT one goal remains constant. According to its mission, the agency strives "...to protect and defend the United States against terrorist and foreign intelligence threats and to enforce the criminal laws of the United States."[1] This holds true for every program in the bureau.

Part of the FBI's National Security Branch, the Counterintelligence Division (CD) protects the United States against the foreign intelligence threats defined in the agency's mission. As with any of the bureau's divisions, CD encounters challenges and often employs its own unique investigative techniques to address them. "It's not just the more traditional spies passing U.S. secrets to foreign governments.... It also involves students and scientists and plenty of other persons stealing the valuable trade secrets of American universities and businesses—the ingenuity that drives our economy—and providing them to other countries. It's nefarious actors sending controlled technologies overseas that help build bombs and weapons of mass destruction designed to hurt and kill Americans and others."[2]

One universal factor generally holds true across all divisions and programs: The FBI accomplishes its challenging mission by developing human sources. To this end, a unique, sophisticated resource exists—the National Center for the Analysis of Violent Crime (NCAVC)—to bolster the agency's criminal and terrorism investigations. The center strives to "...provide behavioral-based operational support to federal, state, local, and international law enforcement agencies involved in the investigation of unusual or repetitive violent crimes, communicated threats, terrorism, and other matters of interest to law enforcement and national security agencies."[3]

NCAVC consists of special agents and other professionals who provide advice and support for cases, including those involving child abductions or mysterious disappearances of children; serial, spree, mass, and other murders; serial rape; extortion; threats; kidnaping; product tampering; arson and bombings; weapons of mass destruction; public corruption; cyber crime; and domestic and international terrorism.[4]

Similarly, CD has its own behavioral team—the Behavioral Analysis Program (BAP), which supports the division's strategic goals by providing direct operational support to counterintelligence investigators. The program provides consultative services from a team of trained and experienced BAP members who review and analyze pertinent behavioral information and develop cogent suggestions and strategies for the interaction between investigators and subjects. The assessment and engagement strategies devised merely result from the thoughtful process of creating a positive interaction and possible relationship between two individuals, whether the goal is an interview, confession, or development of a confidential human source.

Background

Years ago a newly formed cyber crime task force recruited Clark—a senior agent—because of her expertise in developing confidential human sources while resolving terrorism cases. Prior to her assignment on the cyber squad, she developed substantial proactive source-development and rapport-building skills that have served her well throughout her career.[5] Once again, Clark has found herself in a unique learning situation.

Following a recent regional InfraGard meeting, one of Clark's program outreach contacts informed her that the company where she works had an attempted cyber intrusion.[6]

The contact's information security officer stated that the attack originated from overseas and has a possible foreign-government nexus from a country hostile to the United States. Clark thanked the contact and promised that she would look into the matter and be back in touch with her if that was OK. She noted that the contact's shoulders became relaxed and that her facial tension seemed to melt away with the response. The contact thanked Clark and offered to assist in any way possible.

Clark returned to her office, excited about the possibility of a new case—specifically, one with a possible foreign nexus. She had handled many international terrorism cases before beginning her current assignment. Although she relished the cyber task force investigations, Clark sometimes missed the unique challenges of working cases with international implications. Because this was the first time while on the cyber task force that Clark had a lead on a case with a possible foreign-government nexus, she was unsure where to start. She sat in her cubicle, leaned back in her chair while folding her hands behind her head, and stared blankly ahead, pondering her first investigative move. While Clark contemplated her course of action, Smith walked by, noted this familiar look of Clark's, and said, "Hey, what's up?"

Smith—a squad member and friend—and Clark worked together for most of their careers on the terrorism task force before Clark accepted the transfer to the cyber task force. Since then Smith had moved to a counterintelligence squad. He was an experienced agent well-known throughout the division as an effective confidential human source developer and overall behaviorist. Smith is easygoing and has a humility that naturally has people gravitate toward him and tell him their life stories. Since he moved to the counterintelligence squad, the CD BAP team sought him out to be a field assessor/team member because of his background and skills.

Startled from her thoughts, Clark swiveled in her chair and smiled when she saw her friend Smith. "Hey, it's good to see you. How could you tell something was up?" Smith returned the smile and said, "I've seen you with that look hundreds of times in the past. Can I help at all?" Clark pulled up a chair for Smith and explained the potentially exciting new case she had. She also described her uncertainty of where to begin and stated that she was glad he came by.

As Clark recounted the situation, including the potential foreign-government connection, Smith nodded his head as he listened intently. When she finished her explanation, Smith offered, "This sounds like a great case. I recently had a similar one, and I found the National Cyber Investigative Joint Task Force (NCIJTF) a great place to start. It may be for you, as well. It is a multiorganizational task force that assists in situations, like yours. In my last case, it leveraged its participating agencies to jointly identify the person at the other end of the attempted cyber penetration, and we used the resource of the BAP team I am on to create an effective source-development plan."[7] Immediately intrigued, Clark asked her longtime friend and mentor how the BAP creates its strategies.

Behavioral Process

Smith smiled and slightly chuckled as he grabbed a piece of paper from Clark's desk and said, "Just like when we broke down the proactive source development model, as well as rapport-building steps, the process is simple and something you have done your entire life without realizing it. We will take the relationship-development 'art form' and make it a 'paint-by-number' five-step process that you can use proactively in any situation."[8] Clark returned the smile and leaned in to see what Smith was writing.

Step One

Smith began by identifying two important—simple, yet sometimes hard to answer—questions that the BAP starts with: 1) *What* do you want the person to either do or tell you? and 2) Why should *they* do it or tell you? Regarding the first question, he explained that if investigators do not understand their exact objective, they should not start at all. Then, Clark asked Smith why he had emphasized "they" in the second sentence. Smith explained that to truly understand the question, investigators have to understand why the *other persons* think they should do or tell you something, not why *you* think they should.

He could see Clark's brow furrow and that she needed a clearer explanation, so he added, "For example, we once had a case involving an agent who had arrested an espionage subject. The individual admitted to the crime and faced 15 years in jail. He negotiated a plea agreement and agreed—in exchange for a lighter sentence—to cooperate and talk with the FBI openly and honestly about everything he had done. The agent informed the BAP team that, indeed, the subject was 'talking,' but he wasn't saying anything of value and that he hoped the team could help with a strategy. The team started out just like I wrote down here by asking the agent what he wanted the subject to tell him. The agent had a well-planned-out list of information he wanted details about.

Team members then asked the case agent why the subject should tell him those things. The agent replied that the individual would serve his full sentence if he didn't. The BAP team then asked how that was working. The agent replied that it wasn't. The team replied, 'Then, we haven't identified why *he* thinks he should tell you. You have identified why *you* think he should tell you.'"

Nodding, Clark said, "You have to get an understanding of the other individuals and why they think they should speak with you from their perspective and in context of how they see the world." Smith said, "Exactly! That's what the BAP team works on for the case agent." Clark nodded and asked, "OK, so what is the secret?" Smith shook his head and replied, "This is no big secret. The process is the same as what most people use everyday unconsciously when they get a friend to tell them something or do them a favor. The BAP team focuses on the application of psychology combined with practical experience to create influence/leadership strategies, not manipulation."

Clark asked how influence and manipulation differ. Smith explained, "The BAP team regards influence as inducing someone to want to do something they may not otherwise have desired to do. These persons also will continue to have positive feelings about both what they did and the individual for whom they did it.

Manipulation is similar in that you induce people to do something they may not otherwise have done, but it differs in that they later will regret having done it and will have negative feelings toward you for inducing them to do it. The team believes in crafting positive engagements with individuals so that even if the person we seek cooperation from declines, they still will walk away from the engagement feeling better for having met the agent."

Clark agreed that it sounded great and said, "OK, show me how, please." Smith took a second piece of paper and wrote out the next step.

> Psychology/Neuroscience
> +
> Culture/Demographic/Generation
> +
> Individual
> =
> Their Context/How They See the World and the
> Types of People With Whom They Develop Trust

Step Two

Smith explained that to answer the second question in step one, "Why should they tell you or do it for you?" we need to understand as much as we can about the individuals' motivations. This may include persons' needs, wants, desires, aspirations, and dreams—what makes them want to get up in the morning and live for tomorrow. Once we ascertain as much of this information as we can, we then can begin to think about how to craft encounters that focus 100 percent on them and not us." He then wrote out the next course of action.

Step Three
Smith explained that the third step involves ascertaining the individuals' context and how they see and experience the world, as well as what types of persons they prefer to develop trust and rapport with and how. "Team members start with the psychology and neuroscience behind how human beings prefer to interact, develop trust, and build relationships. Overall, we focus on how to get individuals' brains to reward them for engaging with us.

These universal strategies apply to all human beings who fall within the normal range of social development. The team then adds the knowledge of the culture, demographic within that culture, and generation to gain a more specific understanding of how they experience the world and the types of people within their world they prefer to interact with. Finally, the team adds information more specific to the individuals from the second step. Generally, there is a great deal more specific information other than the motivations from step two. Finally, the team assembles the information to better understand the persons' context and perception of the world. Additionally, this knowledge gives us insight into the types of individuals people prefer to develop trust with and how they prefer to be interacted with."

Clark was riveted to Smith's description of the process of what she immediately recognized herself doing in many situations without even realizing it. Smith next wrote out the fourth step.

Step Four

Ensure Interviewees Feel Better for

Having Met You
1)   Make it all about them.
2)   Put their wants and needs ahead of
yours.
3)   Empower them with choices that
will satisfy their wants and needs.
4)   Suspend your own ego and validate
them.

Smith explained that they would keep referring to step
four throughout the entire strategy session. With every
idea the team comes up with, they refer to these
concepts to ensure that the subjects will feel better for
having met the agent and feel that the focus is on
them. Smith explained that these strategies are
techniques that trigger the normal human brain to
think positively about the encounter. Clark again
nodded as Smith wrote the last step.

Step Five
Smith explained that the final step simply combines all
that they learned about the individual to craft the
engagement. The team considers the best person to
conduct the encounter, the best location, the best
time, and, finally, the best way to conduct it. Clark
chuckled when she thought about the list and said to
Smith, "Yes, simple enough, and I just did this
yesterday. My next-door neighbor's dog has been
barking at night.

I didn't want to just go over and bang on the door in
the middle of the night. I didn't want to cause hard
feelings and issues for years to come with my
neighbors. I knew I couldn't push this off on someone
else to do. I thought that speaking to them while they
were gardening might be a better time. I thought I
would bring up the conversation by first
complimenting their dog and ask them what kind of
challenges they have in raising such a great dog. I was

hoping that they would bring up the topic for me." "Perfect!" Smith said. "That is exactly the same process the team does when consulting on cases."

Clark thanked Smith for stopping by and talking to her about her dilemma. She was excited about contacting the NCIJTF and, hopefully, the BAP team with her case.

> Craft the Engagement
> 1) Who
> 2) Where
> 3) When
> 4) How

Conclusion

Regardless of the investigative program, human interaction always will prove crucial for success in the FBI. Whether the interaction is between law enforcement partners, bosses, peers, or the FBI and it's confidential human sources, a positive engagement that leaves the other person feeling positive about the encounter, ultimately, will lead to success. No greater resource aids the FBI in its challenging mission than human beings willing to assist. Regardless of the mission, responsible organizations take the time and consideration to focus on the human element and the great resources available to create positive interactions if they hope to succeed.

> Additional Resources
> Tony Alessandra and Michael J. O'Conner, *The Platinum Rule: Discover the Four Basic Business Personalities and How They Can Lead You to Success* (New York, NY: Warner Books, 1996).
> Terry Burnham and Jay Phelan, *Mean*

Genes: From Sex to Money to Food,
Taming Our Primal Instincts (New York,
NY: Penguin Books, 2000).
Dale Carnegie, *How to Win Friends and*
Influence People (New York, NY: Pocket
Books, 1990).
Robin Dreeke, *It's Not All About Me: The*
Top Ten Techniques for Building Rapport
with Anyone (Virginia: People Formula,
2011).
Robin Dreeke, "It's All About Them:
Tools and Techniques for Interviewing
and Human Source Development," *FBI*
Law Enforcement Bulletin, June 2009,
1-9.
Robin Dreeke and Joe Navarro,
"Behavioral Mirroring in
Interviewing," *FBI Law Enforcement*
Bulletin, December 2009, 1-10.
Robin Dreeke and Kara Sidener,
"Proactive Human Source
Development," *FBI Law Enforcement*
Bulletin, November 2010, 1-9.
Sam Gosling, *Snoop: What Your Stuff*
Says About You (New York, NY: Basic
Books, 2008).
Christopher Hadnagy, *Social*
Engineering: The Art of Human
Hacking (Indianapolis, IN: Wiley
Publishing, Inc., 2011).
Aye Jaye, *The Golden Rule of*
Schmoozing: The Authentic Practice of
Treating Others Well(Naperville, IL:
Sourcebooks, 1997).
Joe Navarro, *What Every Body is*
Saying: An Ex-FBI Agent's Guide to
Speed-Reading People (New York, NY:
Harper Collins, 2008).
John Nolan, *Confidential: Business*

Secrets: Getting Theirs—Keeping Yours (Medford Lakes, NJ: Yardley Chambers, 1996).

Endnotes

[1] Federal Bureau of Investigation, *http://www.fbi.gov/about-us/investigate/what_we_investigate* (accessed April 25, 2013).
[2] Federal Bureau of Investigation, *http://www.fbi.gov/news/stories/2011/november/counterintelligence_110411*(accessed April 25, 2013).
[3] Federal Bureau of Investigation, *http://www.fbi.gov/about-us/cirg/investigations-and-operations-support/investigations-operations-support#cirg_ncavc* (accessed April 25, 2013).
[4] Ibid.
[5] Robin Dreeke and Kara Sidener, "Proactive Human Source Development," *FBI Law Enforcement Bulletin,*November 2010, 1-9; and Robin Dreeke, "Mastering Rapport and Having Productive Conversations," *FBI Law Enforcement Bulletin,* October 2012, 8-17.
[6] InfraGard, an FBI program that began in the Cleveland, Ohio, office in 1996, began as a local effort to gain support from the IT industry and academia for the FBI's efforts in the cyber arena. The program expanded to other FBI offices, and in 1998 the bureau assigned national program responsibility for InfraGard to the former National Infrastructure Protection Center (NIPC) and the Cyber Division in 2003. InfraGard and the FBI have developed a relationship of trust and credibility in the exchange of information concerning terrorism, intelligence, criminal, and security matters. For additional information, see*http://www.fbi.gov/news/stories/2010/march/infragard_030810* (accessed April 25, 2013).

The program is part of the FBI's CI Strategic Alliance Partnership, which strives to "protect U.S. sensitive information, technologies, and, thereby, competitiveness in an age of globalization" and "to foster communication and build awareness through partnerships with key public and private entities by educating and enabling our partners to identify what is at counterintelligence risk and how to protect it." For additional information, see *http://www.fbi.gov/about-us/investigate/counterintelligence/strategic-partnerships* (accessed June 4, 2013).

[7] In 2008, a U.S. presidential mandate made the NCIJTF the focal point for all government agencies to coordinate, integrate, and share information related to all domestic cyber threat investigations. The FBI develops and supports NCIJTF, which includes 19 intelligence and law enforcement agencies working side by side to identify key players and schemes. It strives to leverage the authorities of the participating agencies to most effectively protect the nation form cyber threats. For additional information, see *http://www.fbi.gov/about-us/investigate/cyber/ncijtf* (accessed April 29, 2013).

[8] Dreeke, "Mastering Rapport and Having Productive Conversations"; and Dreeke and Sidener, "Proactive Human Source Development.

DISCUSSION QUESTION

Putting aside the chuckles and grins, how to you think that the five-step process relates to Special Agent Clark's ability to resolve issues surrounding her contact's suspicions of a potential cyber attack (if at all)?

CYBER TERROR

By William L. Tafoya, Ph.D.

November 2011: *FBI Law Enforcement Bulletin*

ANYONE EVER MISQUOTED RECOGNIZES THE IMPORTANCE of context. Wrong assumptions about concepts, words, and phrases easily lead to misunderstanding. In the law enforcement community, officers who use a weapon in the line of duty to defend themselves or innocent bystanders may kill but not murder. Context often serves as the crucial variable justifying the use of deadly force. Murder is always killing, but killing is not always murder. Similarly, accurate knowledge of the context and targets of cyber attacks enhances clarity and helps to avoid obscuring intent.

"Cyber terrorism is a component of information warfare, but information warfare is not...cyber terrorism. For this reason, it is necessary to define these topics as separate entities."[1] Said another way, undefined and misunderstood terms easily could lead a conversation to proceed along parallel lines rather than an intersecting track. Thus, differentiating concepts and terms is important, as in the case of understanding what cyber terror is and what it is not.

Information Warfare

Dorothy Denning, one often-cited expert, describes but does not define information warfare (IW): "Information warfare consists of offensive and defensive operations against information resources of a 'win-lose' nature." Further, "Information warfare is about operations that target or exploit information resources."[2] Nevertheless, several secondary and tertiary sources term her description "Denning's Definition."[3] Other researchers assert that "Information warfare is combat operations in a high-tech battlefield environment in which both sides use information technology means, equipment, or systems in a rivalry over the power to obtain, control, and use information."[4]

IW has several variants. Electronic warfare (EW), primarily a military term, is older than IW and dates back to World War II. Information operations (IO) is the more contemporary military nomenclature. EW and IO both are synonymous with IW. None of the three, however, are synonymous with cyber terror. IW, EW, and IO encompass the use of cryptography (cryptology and cryptanalysis), radar jamming, high-altitude aerial reconnaissance, electronic surveillance, electronically acquired intelligence, and steganography. Cyber terrorists may use these same tools. The distinction, however, is not the technological tools employed but the context and target.

In 1991 during Operation Desert Storm, coalition forces used IW, EW, and IO through the clandestine introduction of viruses and logic bombs into Iraqi Republican Guard (IRG) command-and-control-center computers and peripherals, causing the disruption and alteration of the targeting and launching of Scud missiles.[5] Military combatants engaging one another on the battlefield constitutes IW, EO, and IO. Attacking the largely civilian critical infrastructure is not warfare, but terrorism—cyber terror. But, how does cyber terror differ from IW, EW, and IO?

Cyber Terror

The term was coined in the 1980s by Barry Collin who discussed this dynamic of terrorism as transcendence from the physical to the virtual realm and "the intersection, the convergence of these two worlds...."[6] The Center for Strategic and International Studies (CSIS) has defined it as "the use of computer network tools to shut down critical national infrastructures (e.g., energy, transportation, government operations) or to coerce or intimidate a government or civilian population."[7] The author defines cyber terror as "the intimidation of civilian enterprise through the use of high technology to bring about political, religious, or ideological aims, actions that result in disabling or deleting critical infrastructure data or information."

As an illustration in size, this article does not compare to the holdings of the Library of Congress. The loss of the former would be traumatic to the author, but would impact few other people. Loss of the latter, likely irreplaceable, would prove devastating if a cyber attack deleted those files. Of course, neither could compare to the loss of one human life. But, if data or information from any of the nation's critical infrastructure databases were attacked and destroyed, that certainly would impact quality of life.

One expert asserted that if people wanted to know how much to spend on information security, they should calculate the cost of replacing their hard drives and databases in the event they became intentionally wiped out—then, double that estimate.[8] Recently, a graduate student observed that "Cyber terrorism is a critical threat to national security and public policy. The intelligence community (IC) is at a turning point because it is difficult to catch a criminal who establishes an identity in cyberspace. Further, [we are at] a critical point in [time] for public policy because the government will have to devise regulations of electronic data transfer for public, as well as private, information that can be identified and accessed via the Internet."[9]

Although some experts assert that no credible evidence exists that terrorists have initiated cyber attacks, groups, such as Hamas and Hezbollah, allegedly undertook such attacks more than a decade ago.[10] "Lone wolves" have perpetrated more recent ones. The highest levels of government have emphasized the need to focus on this specter.[11]

What are the most vulnerable targets of cyber terrorists? What constitutes the significance of the targets and the magnitude of the threat? Does it matter what the threat is called? Does cyber terror constitute an element of computer crime?

Computer Crime
More than a half century later, not even the most prominent authorities have reached a consensus about what constitutes computer crime. According to one of the pioneers of this genre, the earliest occurrence of such abuse occurred in 1958.[12] The first prosecution under federal law, the Computer Fraud and Abuse Act, Title 18, Section 1030, U.S. Code, was of Robert Tappan Morris, Jr., then a graduate student of computer science, who unleashed the so-called Internet Worm in 1988.[13]

Along the time continuum, this is where the line begins to blur between "conventional" computer crime and what the author refers to as cyber terror. This genus includes the Melissa Virus (1999), ILOVEYOU Virus (2001), Code Red Worm (2002), Blaster Virus (2004), and Conficker Worm (2008). These attacks differ from extortion, fraud, identify theft, and various scams, all of which certainly are malicious. However, acts of cyber terror as here defined impact society— even the nation—not just an individual, elements of the business sector, or government agencies.

Space limitations do not allow for an incident-by-incident accounting of cyber terror episodes. One example is the case of U.S. v. Mitra. In 2003, Rajib K. Mitra undertook an ongoing attack on a police emergency radio system. Initially, authorities investigated Mitra's cyber assaults as a violation of Wisconsin state law, but, ultimately, deemed them attacks on the critical infrastructure. The case was prosecuted under federal law (Computer Fraud and Abuse Act). Mitra, a lone wolf, was tried and convicted on March 12, 2004, and later sentenced to 96 months imprisonment.

Subsequently, his appeal failed. U.S. Seventh Circuit Court of Appeals judges ruled unanimously, noting that "it is impossible to fathom why any sane person would think that the penalty for crippling an emergency-communication system on which lives may depend should [not] be higher than the penalty for hacking into a Web site to leave a rude message."[14]

Clearly, law enforcement agencies need to stay well informed about what the experts think. Most contemporary professionals remain cautious. However, if people wait until they have absolute proof positive, it may be too late. The cyber trends seem clear. Over the course of approximately 13 years, both the number and frequency of instances of digital disorder have intensified, and the sophistication and diversity of types of cyber attacks have increased.

One high-profile specialist contended that "stories of terrorists controlling the power grid, or opening dams, or taking over the air traffic control network and colliding airplanes, are unrealistic scare stories." He went on to invoke a cost-benefit ratio perspective: "We need to understand the actual risks. Here's the critical question we need to answer: Just how likely is a terrorist attack, and how damaging is it likely to be?"[15]Another authority notes that "threats to the critical infrastructure are becoming increasingly frequent" and goes on to say, "Cyber attacks are one of the greatest threats to international peace and security in the 21st Century."[16] Where there is smoke, is fire not obviously far behind? And, what about the future? What technological innovations will impact the ability to serve and protect in the near-term future?

Tomorrow's Challenges
Concerning the use of the term cyber terror, do experts resemble the proverbial blind men who feel different parts of the same elephant? On the near-term horizon, technological wonders will arise of which the unscrupulous will avail themselves, just as others before them have done.[17] But, where do vulnerabilities lie, and what technological tools will terrorists use?

SCADA Systems
Not the only concern, but certainly a major worry, are supervisory control and data acquisition (SCADA) systems. Closely related are digital control systems (DCS) and programmable logic controllers (PLC). SCADA systems are more ubiquitous than personal computers and laptops combined. Without onsite human intervention, they automatically and remotely collect data from sensors in devices used for industrial processing. They store information in databases for subsequent central-site management and processing. SCADA systems have existed since the 1960s.

In the early days, they were stand-alone, and few were networked. Today, virtually all are accessed via the Internet. This may be great as a cost-cutting measure, but not from an information security perspective. Quietly and without fanfare, SCADA systems have proliferated rapidly—for starters, in the electric, oil, and gas; water treatment; waste management; and maritime, air, railroad, and automobile traffic control industries. SCADA systems also are embedded in "telephone and cell phone networks, including 911 emergency services."[18]

These obscure little drone-like computer systems have virtually no security, firewalls, routers, or antivirus software to protect them. They are spread far and wide across the nation, even in some of the most remote places imaginable.[19] One anonymous hacker interviewed for a television program said, "SCADA is a standard approach toward control systems that pervades everything from water supply to fuel lines." He goes on to describe that the systems run operating systems that make them vulnerable.[20]

Ominous Threats
Electromagnetic pulse (EMP) bombs and high-energy radio frequency (HERF) weapons differ from the malicious codes, computer viruses, and worms of yesteryear. While the latter remain worrisome, EMP and HERF are serious menacing perils of the near-term technological age. EMP devices are compact, and perpetrators can use them to overload computer circuitry. These devices can destroy a computer's motherboard and permanently, irretrievably erase data in memory storage devices.[21] Like EMPs, HERF devices use electromagnetic radiation.[22] They, too, deliver heat, mechanical, or electrical energy to a target. The difference is that individuals can focus HERF devices on a specific target using a parabolic reflector.[23]HERF, as asserted, does not cause permanent damage—EMP does.[24] An array of demonstrations of the power of such homemade devices is depicted at several Web sources, such as YouTube.

Bots

Two decades ago, an expert warned about Internet agents, including bots (robots), Web crawlers, Web spiders, and Web scutters, software apps that traverse the Internet while undertaking repetitive tasks, such as retrieving linked pages, specified words or phrases, or e-mail addresses.[25] Although bots have served benign functions—for example, harvesting e-mail addresses—for many years, they now loom large as a near-term future IC and policing issue. More recent research supports this contention. Given these forecasts, the question is not what might happen tomorrow, but, rather, how well-prepared law enforcement will be to protect and serve.

Implications for Law Enforcement

Federal agencies responsible for investigating terrorism, including cyber terror, must remain vigilant. This includes ensuring adequate funding for staffing, equipment, and training. But, beyond that, local law enforcement officers must encourage citizens to be alert and to report suspicious behavior. Many local law enforcement agencies have had useful resources, such as citizens' police academies, for decades. These programs can educate taxpayers about activity in the physical realm that should be reported. However, what about transcendence to the virtual realm? Since 1996, the FBI's InfraGard Program, an information sharing and analysis effort, has focused on marshaling the talents of members of America's information security (INFOSEC) community.[26] However, what of "main street USA"?

See Something, Say Something is a terrific crime prevention slogan promoted in New York City.[27] It seems to have resonated recently in Times Square when an observant man, a street vendor and Vietnam veteran, alerted the New York Police Department to the SUV used in what turned out to be, fortunately, a failed Taliban-sponsored car-bombing attempt.[28] Any such program should be augmented to provide to its participants examples of behavior in the business community, including those in a work environment, that could alert authorities to precursors of potential cyber misdeeds. Just as someone does not need specialized education to recognize threats in real life, anyone can recognize these digital threats. One authority notes that "an example of suspicious behavior might be a bit of malicious program attempting to install itself from opening an office document."

To reduce the threat, employees could add a "'behavior' layer to [antivirus products]."[29] Of course, this suggestion could unnerve many civil liberty-oriented watchdog organizations; there is no reason not to include such agencies in the discussion, planning, and implementation of the augmentation here proposed. What, then, is the bottom line?

Necessary Preparations
Earthquakes, hurricanes, tsunamis, tornadoes, volcanoes, toxic spills, forest fires, and shark attacks do not occur with great frequency. Precautions, nevertheless, are in place to protect people from the physical threats posed when these natural but seldom-occurring violent events occur. Although they cannot be forecast with great accuracy, we are prepared for them. Similarly, law enforcement agencies should be prepared to deal with the aftermath of hard-to-forecast, but not regularly reoccurring, cyber attacks on the nation's critical infrastructure.

Criminals are menacing our cyber shores, preparing to launch a large-scale attack. What is clear is that it will happen. What is not obvious is by whom or when. Respected INFOSEC authorities have made a compelling case for the "swarm"—attacks via different paths by dispersed cells. Al Qaeda already has demonstrated an understanding of the technique.[30] Other countries, such as India, Saudi Arabia, China, France, Brazil, and Spain, already have experienced such attacks.[31] Additionally, well-known U.S. companies have reported major breaches targeting source code.[32]

Cyber terrorists are pinging ports and probing our digital fortifications as they endeavor to identify vulnerabilities. Daily crackers and terrorists are skulking, battering firewalls, and learning more each time they do so. Clearly, preparations to thwart such attacks are necessary.

Conclusion
The skills, tools, and techniques are the same, but information warfare is conducted between military combatants; cyber terrorism targets civilians. Cyber terrorists indiscriminately will attack the nation's critical infrastructure and civilians—the innocent. Thus, the context and targets, not the technological tools or frequency of attacks, are the more appropriate delimiters that distinguish cyber terror from information warfare.

Some of these criminals are being caught and prosecuted, but more remain undetected. To best serve its motto, "to protect and serve," law enforcement must proactively guard this country's national security on every front.

Endnotes
[1] Robert Taylor, Eric Fritsch, Tory Caeti, Kall Loper, and John Liederbach, *Digital Crime and Digital Terrorism* (Upper Saddle River, NJ: Pearson Prentice Hall, 2011), 19.
[2] Dorothy Denning, *Information Warfare and Security* (Reading, MA: Addison-Wesley Longman, 1999), 21.
[3] Maura Conway, "Cyberterrorism: Hype and Reality,"

in *Information Warfare: Separating Hype from Reality*, ed. E. Leigh Armistead (Washington, DC: Potomac Books, 2007), 73–93.

4 Wang Baocun and Li Fei, "Information Warfare," Academy of Military Science, Beijing, China, *http://www.fas.org/irp/world/china/docs/iw_wang. htm* (accessed October 28, 2010).

5 Denning; and Alvin and Heidi Toffler, *War and Anti-War: Survival at the Dawn of the 21st Century*(Boston, MA: Little, Brown, 1993).

6 Barry Collin, "The Future of Cyberterrorism," *Crime & Justice International Journal* (March 1997): 15.

7 James Lewis, "Assessing the Risks of Cyber Terrorism, Cyber War and Other Cyber Threats," Center for Strategic and International Studies, *http://csis.org/files/media/csis/pubs/021101_ris ks_of_cyberterror.pdf*(accessed October 28, 2010).

8 Dr. Grace Hopper, "Future of Computing" (lectures, FBI Academy, Quantico, VA, 1985-1991). See also*http://www.sdsc.edu/ScienceWomen/hopper.html* (acce ssed October 29, 2010);*http://www.youtube.com/watch?v=7sUT7gFQEsY* (ac cessed October 29, 2010); and*http://www.youtube.com/watch?v=CVMhPVInxoE&feat ure=related* (accessed October 29, 2010).

9 Mehwish Salim, "Cyber Terror: Unequivocal Threat or Hyperbole?" (award-winning paper presentation, 34th Annual Meeting of the Northeastern Association of Criminal Justice Sciences, Bristol, RI, June 9-12, 2010).

10 David Pettinari, "Cyber Terrorism-Information Warfare in Every Hamlet," *Police Futurist 5*, no. 3 (1997): 7-8.

11 National Security Council, "The Comprehensive National Cybersecurity Initiative,"*http://www.globalsecurity.org/security/library/p olicy/national/cnci_2010.htm* (accessed October 29, 2010); and CBS, "Sabotaging the System," 60 Minutes, *http://video.techrepublic.com.com/2422- 13792_11-364499.html* (accessed October 29 2010).

12 Donn Parker, *Crime by Computer* (New York, NY: Charles Scribner's Sons, 1976).

13 Ronald Standler, "Computer Crime," *http://www.rbs2.com/ccrime.htm* (accessed October 29, 2010).

14 U.S. v. Mitra 04-2328.

15 Bruce Schneier, *Beyond Fear: Thinking Sensibly About Security in an Uncertain World* (New York, NY: Copernicus Books, 2003).

16 Jeffrey Carr, *Inside Cyber Warfare* (Sebastopol, CA: O'Reilly, 2010).

17 For more information, visit *http://www.battelle.org*.

18 Gregory Coates, "Collaborative, Trust-Based Security Mechanisms for a National Utility Intranet" (master's thesis, Air Force Institute of Technology, 2007).

19 William Graham, Chairman, Critical National Infrastructures, "Report of the Commission to Assess the Threat to the United States from Electromagnetic Pulse (EMP) Attack," EMP Commission,*http://empcommission.org/docs/A2473-EMP_Commission-7MB.pdf*(accessed October 29, 2010); Seth Fogie, "SCADA and Security,"*http://www.informit.com/guides/content.aspx?g=security&seqNum=322* (accessed October 29, 2010); and Seth Fogie, "SCADA In-Security,"*http://www.informit.com/guides/content.aspx?g=security&seqNum=323* (accessed October 29, 2010).

20 Tom Longstaff, "Cyberwar: Vulnerability of Scada Systems?"*http://www.pbs.org/wgbh/pages/frontline/shows/cyberwar/vulnerable/scada.html* (accessed October 29, 2010).

21 Graham.

22 For additional information, see *http://www.lbl.gov/MicroWorlds/ALSTool/EMSpec/* (accessed October 29, 2010).

23 For additional information, see *http://www.wordiq.com/definition/Parabolic_reflector* (accessed October 29, 2010).

24 John Geis, "Directed Energy Weapons of the Battlefield: A New Vision for 2025" (paper, Center for Strategy and Technology, Air War University, Maxwell Air Force Base, Alabama, 2003).

25 Kevin Manson, "Robots, Wanderers, Spiders and Avatars: The Virtual Investigator and Community Policing Behind the Thin Digital Blue Line" (presentation, annual meeting of the Academy of Criminal Justice Sciences, Louisville, KY, March 15, 1997).

26 For more information, visit *http://www.infragard.net*.

27 For more information,
visit *http://www.mta.info/mta/security/index.html.*
28 "President Calls to Thank Times Square
Vendor," *Associated Press*, May 2, 2010; and Anne
Komblut,"Pakistani Taliban Behind Attempted Times
Square Car Bombing, Attorney General Says,"*Washington
Post*, May 9, 2010.
29 Frances Alonzo, "Security Expert Urges Shift in Tactics
Against Cyber Attacks,"*http://it.moldova.org/news/
security-expert-urges-shift-in-tactics-against-cyber-attacks-
206747-eng.html* (accessed October 29, 2010).
30 John Arquilla and David Ronfeldt, *Swarming and the
Future of Conflict* (Santa Monica, CA: RAND, 2000); and
John Arquilla and David Ronfeldt, "Fighting the Network
War," *Wired* 9, no. 12 (2001).
31 Kim Zetter, "Google Hackers Targeted Source Code of
More Than 30 Companies,"
http://www.wired.com/threatlevel/2010/01/google-hack-
attack/ (accessed October 29, 2010).
32 Kim Zetter, "Report: Critical Infrastructures Under
Constant Cyberattack
Globally"*http://www.wired.com/threatlevel/2010/01/csis-
report-on-cybersecurity/* (accessed October 29, 2010).

DISCUSSION QUESTION

Similar to the laser attacks described in a previous article, what do you think motivates individuals to intentionally harm computer programs, computers, networks, and businesses?

STATEMENT BEFORE THE HOUSE COMMITTEE ON
HOMELAND SECURITY, SUBCOMMITTEE ON
COUNTERTERRORISM AND INTELLIGENCE

By C. Frank Figliuzzi

Assistant Director, Counterintelligence Division
Federal Bureau of Investigation

June 2012: *FBI Law Enforcement Bulletin*

GOOD MORNING CHAIRMAN MEEHAN, RANKING MEMBER Higgins, and members of the Subcommittee. Thank you for the opportunity to testify before you today. For the past year and a half, I have had the privilege of leading the FBI's Counterintelligence Division (CD). Our mission is to identify, disrupt, and defeat the efforts of foreign intelligence services operating inside the United States. In the FBI's pending case load for the current fiscal year, economic espionage losses to the American economy total more than $13 Billion.

The health of America's companies is vital to our economy, and our economy is a matter of national security. But the FBI, with our partners, is making strides in disrupting economic espionage plots. In just the last four years, the number of arrests the FBI has made associated with economic espionage has doubled; indictments have increased five-fold; and convictions have risen eight-fold. In just the current fiscal year, the FBI has made 10 arrests for economic espionage related charges; federal courts have indicted 21 of our subjects (including indictments of five companies), and convicted nine defendants. In the current fiscal year so far, we have already surpassed the statistics recorded for FY 2011 and expect them to continue to rise. With each year, foreign intelligence services and their collectors become more creative and more sophisticated in their methods to undermine American business and erode the one thing that most provides American business its leading edge; our ability to innovate.

As the FBI's economic espionage caseload is growing, so is the percentage of cases attributed to an insider threat, meaning that, individuals currently (or formerly) trusted as employees and contractors are a growing part of the problem.

According to a February 2012 indictment, several former employees with more than 70 combined years of service to the company were convinced to sell trade secrets to a competitor in the People's Republic of China (PRC). Entities owned by the PRC government sought information on the production of titanium dioxide, a white pigment used to color paper, plastics, and paint.

The PRC government tried for years to compete with DuPont Corporation, which holds the largest share of a $12 billion annual market in titanium dioxide. Five individuals and five companies were commissioned by these PRC state-owned enterprises collaborate in an effort to take DuPont's technology to the PRC and build competing titanium dioxide plants, which would undercut DuPont revenues and business. Thus far, three co-conspirators have been arrested and one additional co-conspirator has pled guilty in federal court. This case is one of the largest economic espionage cases in FBI history. The insider threat, of course, is not new, but it's becoming more prevalent for a host of reasons, including:

- The pervasiveness of employee financial hardships during economic difficulties;
- The global economic crisis facing foreign nations, making it even more attractive,
- cost-effective, and worth the risk to steal technology rather than invest in research
- and development;
- The ease of stealing anything stored electronically, especially when one has
- legitimate access to it; and
- The increasing exposure to foreign intelligence services presented by the reality of global business, joint ventures, and the growing international footprint of American firms.

To address the evolving insider threat, the FBI has become more proactive to prevent losses of information and technology. CD continues expanding our outreach and liaison alliances to government agencies, the defense industry, academic institutions, and, for the first time, to the general public, because of an increased targeting of unclassified trade secrets across all American industries and sectors.

On May 11, 2012, the FBI launched a media campaign highlighting the insider threat relating to economic espionage. This campaign included print and television interviews, billboards along busy commuter corridors in nine leading research areas nationwide, and public information on the FBI website. Through this campaign, the FBI hopes to reach the public and business communities by explaining how the insider threat affects a company's operations and educating them on how to detect, prevent, and respond to threats to their organizations' proprietary information. Perhaps the most important among these is identifying and taking defensive measures against employees stealing trade secrets.

A recent case underscores the value of the FBI and private companies working together to stop economic espionage and prevent financial losses or breaches of national security. An employee at a Utah company noticed a co-worker download the recipe for manufacturing a proprietary chemical and email it to his personal email account.

After this suspicious activity was reported, the company opened its own investigation into the matter and learned that the employee had shared the manufacturing secret with an individual associated with a foreign chemical company. Because of an FBI presentation about economic espionage, company executives called the FBI, and the employee was arrested and charged within 10 days. If businesses, universities, and law enforcement continue to partner together, we can track, apprehend, and prosecute many more individuals suspected of economic espionage.

A second grave threat to our national security is the illegal transfer of U.S. technology. The FBI is seeing an expansion of weapons proliferation cases involving US acquired components. These are components exported from American companies, initially headed to someplace they're allowed to be, but ultimately destined for someplace they should never be. The FBI's Counterproliferation Center (CPC), which identifies and disrupts networks of weapons of mass destruction (WMD) activity, is responsible for pursuing cases of illegal technology transfer, whether the technology is intended for WMDs or other uses. The CPC has tripled its disruptions of illegal transfers of technology since FY 2011. We have made more than a dozen arrests since the CPC's inception in July 2011, including the arrests of multiple subjects on the Central Intelligence

Agency's Top Ten Proliferators List. The CPC has also surpassed statistics recorded for FY 2011 and in FY 2012 (to-date).

One example of this sort of case involved an Iranian proliferation network with associates in Hong Kong, Taiwan, Singapore, and Malaysia, and particularly highlights our partnership with the Department of Commerce's Office of Export Enforcement and Homeland Security Investigations. The network leader targeted dual-use electronic equipment including radio frequency modules.

The target obtained this equipment from unwitting U.S. companies and shipped them to intermediary front companies in East Asia before ultimately rerouting the shipments to Iran. Over a dozen of these components have been recovered in caches of improvised explosive devices (IEDs) or recovered as part of the remote detonation systems of the pre- and post-blast IEDs used against American soldiers in Iraq from 2008-2011. Four coconspirators in Singapore have been arrested and extradition proceedings to the United States to stand trial are ongoing. One US co-conspirator, who worked in research and development at the company manufacturing and shipping these items, pled guilty in federal court this January.

The answer to the threat lies, in part, on the partnerships represented at this hearing. Acting together, we are stronger than when we act alone and are producing results. As we continue our investigative and prosecutorial efforts we make it more painful for individuals and entities to carry out missions related to economic espionage. And as we strengthen and expand public awareness of the threat through our alliances with business and academia, we harden our defenses against those who would do us harm. Again, thank you for the opportunity to speak with you today. I would be pleased to answer any questions.

DISCUSSION QUESTIONS

Similar indeed to the article on Economic Espionage, the FBI cites this case as one of its largest in this regard. It is one thing to steal corporate or national secrets from abroad via a computer system, but it is quite another to attempt to purchase secrets from corporate or government employees. From a behavioral perspective, what do you think American companies can do in an effort to prevent and/or identify employees who might be inclined or otherwise predisposed to participate in such nefarious acts?

CRITICAL THINKING EXERCISE

Undertake some preliminary research (open source, of course) to ascertain what other agencies of the U.S. government are doing in terms of combating economic espionage. Agencies you should look at could include: Immigration and Customs Enforcement (ICE), Defense Criminal Investigative Service (DCIS), Air Force Office of Special Investigations (OSI) and Naval Criminal Investigative Service (NCIS).

THE SPYING GAME
TRICKS OF TODAY'S TRADE

July 2007: *FBI Law Enforcement Bulletin*

O NE OF YOUR EXECS IS ON A BUSINESS TRIP OVERSEAS. At an opportune time, a foreign spy covertly plants software on her laptop. Unsuspecting, she returns home and plugs her laptop into your company's computer network. By the time your security experts get wind of it, your most cherished business secrets are long gone.

Welcome to the twenty-first century world of espionage. Threats like these may sound like the stuff of fiction, but they are real and could well be coming to a factory, office, or university near you.

But there's some good news. Armed with an understanding of the possibilities, you can minimize the risk of you and your organization becoming an unwitting target.

So what do you need to know? Here are some basics.

Know What Spies Want
At the top of their country's hit lists:

- The inside skinny on our government's policies and intentions towards their country.

- Details on U.S. military plans and weapons systems.
- The crown jewels of our economy: our nation's best scientific and technological innovations and research, both public and private.
- Cutting edge U.S. management practices, which themselves are a valuable asset.

Know Their Favorite "Disguises"

- Representatives at supposed "research institutes";
- Visiting business professionals and scientists who want to tour your state-of-the-art plants and operations worldwide (a great place to take pictures and make friends);
- Tourists or visitors on non-immigrant visas;
- Diplomatic officials, the standard cover;
- False front companies; and
- Students and educators.

Know Their Collection Strategies
Here are just a few you might not expect:

- Out of the blue, you get a call asking for the latest manual for one of your products. Or someone shows up unannounced at your plant and asks to buy large quantities of your electronics. The end game? They dissect your products and then go out and start producing the technologies themselves.

- You hire a foreign-born engineer who has been educated in this country. Over a 10-15 year period, she rises to mid-level management. Then, she returns to her home country—where she gets paid by that government to set up a business that competes with yours.

- A series of university students and professors from overseas take jobs in research labs on campus and get involved in related military projects. Individually, they learn only bits and pieces. But collectively, when they pass that information back to their home country, it paints a telling picture of our country's defense initiatives.

- Foreign intelligence operatives strike up a relationship with a business professional, tourist, diplomat, expatriate, or student visiting their country. At first, it's a purely social relationship. But then it slowly turns to talk of what that person may know. In some cases, that person may end up selling vital secrets for cash.

CRITICAL THINKING EXERCISE

This short article definitely hits the nail on the head as to what corporate and foreign spies want. But after interviewing and interrogating many operative—including double agents—there is one thing that is left off this list! And that is information that can be used to extort U.S. government officials and/or corporate executives. In outline form, describe what information of this type such agents would be after, and how they might accomplish their goals. Finally, come up with a short list of what officials can do to prevent such occurrences, and further, how they might be able to identify if colleagues are being extorted for money and/or secrets.

Social Network Analysis
A Systematic Approach for Investigating

By Jennifer A. Johnson, Ph.D.,
John David Reitzel, Ph.D., Bryan F. Norwood,
David M. McCoy, D. Brian Cummings,
and Renee R. Tate

March 2013: *FBI Law Enforcement Bulletin*

SOCIAL NETWORK ANALYSIS (SNA) IS OFTEN CONFUSED with social networking sites, such as Facebook, when in fact, SNA is an analytical tool that can be used to map and measure social relations. Through quantitative metrics and robust visual displays, police can use SNA to discover, analyze, and visualize the social networks of criminal suspects.

SNA, a social science methodology, serves as a valuable tool for law enforcement. While technologically sophisticated, SNA proves easy to employ. Using available data, police departments structure the examination of an offender's social network in ways not previously possible.

Manual examination of social networks tends to be difficult, time consuming, and arbitrary, making it more prone to error. SNA provides a systematic approach for investigating large amounts of data on people and relationships. It improves law enforcement effectiveness and efficiency by using complex information regarding individuals socially related to suspects. This often leads to improved clearance rates for many crimes and development of better crime prevention strategies.

SNA derives its value from human organization and social interaction for criminal and noncriminal purposes. Social networks sometimes promote illegal behavior (e.g., juvenile delinquency and gang-related crime) among related offenders across criminal domains. They can provide a source for illicit drug and pornography distribution and international terrorism.[1] The networks may supply an essential first condition for many serious criminal behaviors.

Social networks that enable crime are not mutually exclusive from the networks of law- abiding citizens. They are interspersed within these communities, drawing support from residents and extracting significant costs from host neighborhoods.[2] The influence of social networks in producing criminal behavior indicates that effective crime-fighting strategies are contingent upon law enforcement's ability to identify and respond appropriately to the networks where the behavior is embedded.

THEORY AND METHOD

SNA is a theory about how humans organize and a method to examine such organization. The approach indicates that actors are positioned in and influenced by a larger social network. Methodologically, it provides a precise, quantitative tool through which agencies can identify, map, and measure relationship patterns.

Three points of data—two actors and the tie or link between them—comprise the basic unit of analysis. Actors "nodes" are people, organizations, computers, or any other entity that processes or exchanges information or resources. Relationships "ties, connections, or edges" between nodes represent types of exchange, such as drug transactions between a seller and buyer, phone calls between two terrorists, or contacts between victims and offenders. SNA focuses on both positive and negative relationships between sets of individuals.

This analysis produces two forms of output, one visual and the other mathematical. The visual consists of a map or rendering of the network, called a social network diagram, which displays the nodes and relationships between them. In larger networks, key nodes are more difficult to identify; therefore, the analysis turns to the quantitative output of SNA.

The centrality of nodes, such as those representing offenders, identifies the prominence of persons to the overall functioning of the network. It indicates their importance to the criminal system, role, level of activity, control over the flow of information, and relationships. Basic centrality metrics provide further details. "Degree" gauges how many connections a particular node possesses, "betweenness" measures how important it is to the flow, and "closeness" indicates how quickly the node accesses information from the network. Nodes are rank ordered according to their centrality, with those at the top playing the most prominent role. These measures cannot tell an analyst what the structure should be, but they can elaborate on the actual makeup of the network. The value and actionable intelligence of each of these metrics is determined by the information the analyst wants.

CASE STUDY
In January 2008 a collaborative pilot project was launched to explore the viability of incorporating SNA into the precinct-level crime analysis methodologies of the Richmond, Virginia, Police Department (RPD).

Participants included representatives of RPD, a university sociologist, and a software designer. The goal was for the research team, comprised of the sociologist and the software designer, to use crime data to assess how constructive SNA would be in solving the most prevalent crimes in the area and to determine the feasibility of training the precinct-level analysts to incorporate it into their workflow.

Researchers needed to determine what initiated violence between two groups of previously friendly young males. Several persons of interest, at one time on good terms, began to argue and assault one another. The source of the violence was not clear, and police were looking for ways to respond. They wanted to know if SNA could help them understand what sparked the violence and which strategies could be developed using a network approach.

The research team received access to RPD's records management system to obtain information on criminal occurrences, arrests, criminal associates, demographics, and victim/offender relationships. The police provided no other background information on the individuals. The research team did not meet or discuss the ongoing investigation with the detectives. Analysis was done off-site, and the only recurring contact was with the police manager to extract the data in relational form.

Using 24 persons of interest labeled by a gang unit detective as "seeds"—starting points, or initially identified persons—the records management system extracted all connections among the seeds from 2007 through October 2008, proceeding four layers out and including any interconnections among the seed and nodes in each step. The connections were categorized by incident type—common incident participation, victim/offender, gang memberships, field contacts, involved others, common locations, and positive or negative connections.

Positive ties included a cooperative relationship between individuals, such as having family connections, robbing a store together, or hanging out. Negative ties indicated hostile relationships, such as those between a victim and offender. Individuals could have multiple and varying connections. Four networks resulted from the sampling, one for each layer out from the seeds. The networks included the seeds, the relationships among them, people directly connected to them, and those related to their associates. This involved 434 individuals and 1,711 ties. Several weak spots existed where a single node connected regions of the network and indicated dense areas of heavy interconnectivity.

Using SNA software, an analyst quickly produced a visual representation, including names, to assess the structure of the group or reference to whom a person of interest was connected. Through visual analysis and examination of the metric of betweenness, analysts located the source of the disagreement. The metric pointed to critical junctures in the network that revealed interpersonal tensions among males revolving around their relationships with females.

Two powerful male gang members reportedly had a positive relationship in October of 2007; however, in April 2008, one victimized a female friend of the other. During the same incident, this male also victimized the female friend of another male. Throughout the episode, a pattern emerged involving situations where a dominant male engaged with a female associate of another strong male. In other words, boys were fighting over girls.

Quantitative metrics provided additional information identifying the powerful players in this network. By rank ordering the individuals according to their centrality measures, the analysis confirmed that the gang unit was watching the right people and using community resources effectively. The metrics also helped unit members further analyze the importance of the seed nodes. Many of the nodes targeted by the unit ranked as powerful in the network based on an SNA metric. The quantitative metrics indicated six other vital players, including one critical to the flow of the network.

RESULTS
Unanticipated administrative processes delayed the timeline of the pilot project, making these results and recommendations too late to be actionable. The police already had solved the conflict. The knowledge of the detectives, which the research team was not privy to, validated the results. Officers confirmed that the answer the research team had discerned from the data—boys fighting over girls—was the cause of the conflict.

Detectives acknowledged that they would have solved the case more quickly and easily if they had this analysis available to guide their strategies. This feedback validated the worth of the approach and the usefulness of SNA and moved the project into the next phase. Precinct-level crime analysts received training in SNA through a 36-hour, in-house seminar. Through lectures and hands-on training, crime analysts from police and federal agencies used data from their own projects to learn to incorporate SNA to meet their needs. Within 2 weeks of completing the course, the analysts used SNA in several cases, including an aggravated assault/ shooting and several convenience store robberies.

In the shooting incident, the analyst used SNA to provide data on an associate of the suspect who previously was not noticed by the detective working the case. The analyst provided that information to the detective who used it to locate and interview that individual, which put additional pressure on the suspect, who was attempting to elude capture. This, combined with other social and financial pressures, caused the suspect to surrender.

Another case involved a string of convenience store robberies. Using an SNA map of a separate case, an analyst noticed a connection between a person of interest in the robberies in one precinct and a member of the network under investigation. Using the two names as seeds, the analyst extracted another previously unknown network. The analyst and a colleague identified one of the seed names as a person of interest in robberies involving multiple juveniles. Through cooperation and an SNA social diagram, they pieced together robberies not previously thought to be connected and identified a suspect involved in other robberies. The chart provided a source where they quickly, easily, and effectively could share observations with investigative personnel.

SOCIAL NETWORK DIAGRAMS
Social network diagrams have become a method for RPD to use social relationships among offenders and their associates. Renowned for its technological innovation and policing strategies, RPD has found SNA effective in facilitating better communication between crime analysts and investigators. SNA enabled the department to significantly increase crime clearance rates and reduce violence.

Prior to the SNA training, analysts conceptualized a series of "star" networks with an "ego" at the center and immediate connections radiating out. To understand the network, analysts identified the immediate connections of a person of interest. To identify one of the people connected to the original person of interest, a second ego network was constructed. In the end, the analyst faced a series of networks, leaving out the interconnections between them. Through training, analysts began to interpret the effectiveness of the larger network environment using diagrams as social maps to orient themselves and officers.

In the shooting case, the detective used the network analysis to apply pressure to the suspect by interviewing an associate whose relationship with the offender previously was unknown. Mounting social and financial pressures, ultimately, led the individual to surrender. In the convenience store robberies, an SNA diagram provided vital clues that allowed multiple analysts to share information and identify previously unknown connections between individuals, which led to a possible suspect. If SNA had been available to analysts in other jurisdictions, a connection may have been discovered earlier.

ANALYSIS

The cases described illustrate the success of SNA in developing law enforcement strategies and interdiction techniques. The pilot project demonstrated how SNA can help answer sophisticated questions regarding motivations for a crime—an area previously underdeveloped in crime analysis processes.[3] The research team was asked to determine why violence occurred among groups who previously were amicable. Using visual analysis and without any subject matter knowledge, investigators used SNA to reveal behavioral motivation rooted in complex interpersonal relationships. The project provided confirmation of the effectiveness of the current resource allocation of the gang unit and indicated new avenues of policing, which have the potential to produce a high return on investment.

These two cases produced actionable results, illustrating how SNA can facilitate a productive working relationship between crime analysts and detectives. The academic research on policing indicated that one of the biggest hurdles in establishing effective communication is finding a common language between the analytics of numbers and the immediate pressures of reality.[4] Each case described illustrates how SNA and social network diagrams function as a common ground. Analysts used the charts visually to depict their analysis, which resonated with detectives because it reflected their reality. The analysts provided something new to the detectives, thus, aiding each investigation.

The visual and quantitative output of SNA helps solve institutional memory issues associated with analysts' longevity and attrition, as well as new hires. By producing a current overview, SNA allows new analysts to grasp the present status of the network. It assists experienced analysts in maintaining an understanding of the network by chronicling growth and development as members and connections appear and disappear.

Law enforcement agencies, such as RPD, benefit from having access to structured, relational, and temporal data. Analysts reliably map changes in the network using an automated extraction process. Through this dynamic procedure, experienced analysts appear less likely to develop data analysis blind spots.

CONCLUSION
Law enforcement agencies have come a long way from pinpoint mapping. The technological advancements in recent years can provide personnel more confidence to handle complex crime problems confronting departments around the country. Social network

analysis demonstrated its utility and effectiveness as a means of solving crimes or determining persons of interest and bridging the gap between crime analysts and police officers in the field. With the support of robust technology, SNA becomes reliable across time, data, analysts, and networks and quickly produces actionable results inside any operational law enforcement environment.

ENDTEXT

The authors commend and recognize the Richmond, Virginia, Police Department's Crime Analysis Unit for its critical role and ongoing cooperation in the research and writing of this article.

ENDNOTES

[1] E. Patacchini and Y. Zenou, "The Strength of Weak Ties in Crime," *European Economic Review* 52, no. 2 (2008); D.L. Haynie, "Delinquent Peers Revisited: Does Network Structure Matter?" *American Journal of Sociology* 106, no.4 (2001): 1013-1057; K. Murji, "Markets, Hierarchies, and Networks: Race/Ethnicity and Drug Distribution," *Journal of Drug Issues* 37, no. 4 (2007): 781-804; V. Krebs, "Mapping Networks of Terrorist Cells," *Connections* 24, no. 3 (2004): 43-52; and J.A. Johnson, "To Catch a Curious Clicker: A Social Network Analysis of the Online Commercial Pornography Network" in *Everyday Pornographies*, Karen Boyle, ed. (Routledge Press, 2012).

[2] C. Kadushin, "Who Benefits from Network Analysis: Ethics of Social Network Research" *Social Networks* 27, no. 2 (2005): 139-153.

[3] T.C. O'Shea and K. Nicholls, "Police Crime Analysis: A Survey of U.S. Police Departments with 100 or More Sworn Personnel," *Police Practice and Research* 4, no. 3 (2003): 233-250.

[4] N. Cope, "Intelligence Led Policing or Policing Led Intelligence?" *British Journal of Criminology* 44 (2004): 188-203; and S. Belledin and K. Paletta, "Finding Out What You Don't Know: Tips on Using Crime Analysis," *The Police Chief* 75, no. 9 (2008).

Discussion Questions

Discuss how Social Network Analysis can be used to identify security threats or to assist in undertaking threat assessments.

THE CORPORATE PSYCHOPATH

By

Paul Babiak, Ph.D., and Mary Ellen O'Toole, Ph.D.

November 2012: *FBI Law Enforcement Bulletin*

PSYCHOPATHY IS ONE OF THE MOST STUDIED PERSONALITY disorders. It consists of variations of 20 well-documented characteristics that form a unique human personality syndrome—the psychopath. Many of these traits are visible to those who interact with the psychopath who possess some or all of these characteristics. For some, superficial charm and grandiose sense of self make them likable on first meeting. Their ability to impress others with entertaining and captivating stories about their lives and accomplishments can result in instant rapport. They often make favorable, long-lasting first impressions. This personality disorder is a continuous variable, not a classification or distinct category, which means that not all corporate psychopaths exhibit the same behaviors.

Beneath the cleverly formed façade—typically created by psychopaths to influence their targets—is a darker side, which people eventually may suspect. They can be pathological liars who con, manipulate, and deceive others for selfish means. Some corporate psychopaths thrive on thrill seeking, bore easily, seek stimulation, and play mind games with a strong desire to win. Unlike professional athletes moved by a desire to improve performance and surpass their personal best, psychopaths are driven by what they perceive as their victims' vulnerabilities. Little research exists on their inner psychological experiences; however, they seem to get perverted pleasure from hurting and abusing their victims.

Functional magnetic resonance imaging (FMRI) research indicates that psychopaths are incapable of experiencing basic human emotions and feelings of guilt, remorse, or empathy.[1] This emotional poverty often is visible in their shallow sentiment. They display emotions only to manipulate individuals around them. They mimic other people's emotional responses. Some lack realistic long-term goals, although they can describe grandiose plans. The impulsive and irresponsible psychopath lives a parasitic and predatory lifestyle, seeking out and using other people, perhaps, for money, food, shelter, sex, power, and influence.

Psychopathy is a personality disorder traditionally assessed with the Psychopathy Checklist-Revised (PCL-R).[2] Often used interchangeably with psychopathy, the term *sociopathy* is obsolete and was removed from the Diagnostic and Statistical Manual (DSM) in 1968. Currently, there is no formal diagnosis of psychopathy in the DSM-Fourth Edition-Text Revision (DSM-IV-TR); however, it is being considered for the 2013 DSM-V list of personality disorders.

Façade
It is fascinating that psychopaths can survive and thrive in a corporate environment. Day-to-day interactions with coworkers, coupled with business policies and procedures, should make unmasking them easy, but this does not always hold true. Large

companies' command-and-control functions ought to make dealing with them simple and direct; however, this may not be the case.

Psychopathic manipulation usually begins by creating a mask, known as psychopathic fiction, in the minds of those targeted. In interpersonal situations, this façade shows the psychopath as the ideal friend, lover, and partner. These individuals excel at sizing up their prey. They appear to fulfill their victims' psychological needs, much like the grooming behavior of molesters. Although they sometimes appear too good to be true, this persona typically is too grand to resist. They play into people's basic desire to meet the right person—someone who values them for themselves, wants to have a close relationship, and is different from others who have disappointed them. Belief in the realism of this personality can lead the individual to form a psychopathic bond with the perpetrator on intellectual, emotional, and physical levels. At this point, the target is hooked and now has become a psychopathic victim.

Corporate psychopaths use the ability to hide their true selves in plain sight and display desirable personality traits to the business world. To do this, they maintain multiple masks at length. The façade they establish with coworkers and management is that of the ideal employee and future leader. This can prove effective, particularly in organizations experiencing turmoil and seeking a "knight in shining armor" to fix the company.

Con
How is it possible for psychopaths to fool business-savvy executives and employers? They often use conning skills during interviews to convince their hiring managers that they have the potential for promotion and the knowledge, skills, and abilities to

do an outstanding job. Using their lying skills, they may create phony resumes and fictitious work experience to further their claims. They may manipulate others to act as references. Credentials, such as diplomas, performance awards, and trophies, often are fabricated.

Once inside the organization, corporate psychopaths capitalize on others' expectations of a commendable employee. Coworkers and managers may misread superficial charm as charisma, a desirable leadership trait. A psychopath's grandiose talk can resemble self-confidence, while subtle conning and manipulation often suggest influence and persuasion skills. Sometimes psychopaths' thrill-seeking behavior and impulsivity are mistaken for high energy and enthusiasm, action orientation, and the ability to multitask.

To the organization, these individuals' irresponsibility may give the appearance of a risk-taking and entrepreneurial spirit—highly prized in today's fast-paced business environment. Lack of realistic goal setting combined with grandiose statements can be misinterpreted as visionary and strategic thinking ability; both are rare and sought after by senior management. An inability to feel emotions may be disguised as the capability to make tough decisions and stay calm in the heat of battle.

Damage
Evidence suggests that when participating in teams, corporate psychopaths' behaviors can wreak havoc. In departments managed by psychopaths, their conduct decreases productivity and morale. These issues can have a severe impact on a company's business performance.

There also is the risk for economic crimes to be committed. For the corporate executive and the criminal justice professional, the issue is the possibility of fraud. Today's corporate psychopath may be highly educated—several with Ph.D., M.D., and J.D. degrees have been studied—and capable of circumventing financial controls and successfully passing corporate audits.

Investigation

Investigators should familiarize themselves with the typical traits and characteristics of psychopaths. They must understand the manipulation techniques used to create and manage the psychopathic bonds established with victim organizations. Their reputations, as judged by those in power with whom they have bonded, known as patrons, often provide added protection from closer investigation. As a result, the investigator may need to build a case with management for the use and broad application of more sophisticated techniques.

Psychopaths can be expert liars often immune to traditional deception-revealing techniques. Some practice avoiding detection in anticipation of being caught and interrogated. Therefore, investigators independently should corroborate any information provided by these individuals.[3]

Psychopaths often compartmentalize their behavior, enabling them to present themselves differently to various people. This can help them hide their manipulation and control over victims. Coworkers may have knowledge or suspicions about the psychopath's actions that can be useful to the investigator. However, they either may fear repercussions or fall under the influence of the psychopathic bond. If investigators establish rapport and trust with coworkers, information that will make their work easier may be forthcoming. The difficulty comes when these associates are persons of interest. Fortunately, some companies have hotlines for employees to report coworker fraud and other complaints. This information provides an invaluable source of leads.

Corporate psychopaths with exceptional verbal skills make crafty interviewees. This ability provides an opportunity embraced by many of them to fool law enforcement officers. In these cases, investigators should proceed with caution.[4] Specific interview strategies should focus on exposing psychopaths' vulnerabilities. Possession of a sense of superiority and lack of empathy can enable them to boast about the brilliance of their latest fraud scheme. They often believe that only someone equal in intelligence to them could understand their actions. Strategies specifically designed to elicit such boasting can result in a wealth of information for the investigator.

Corporate psychopaths are successful because they single out and isolate their targets. They sometimes manipulate several victims at the same time. Investigators never should assume they are immune to a psychopath's approach. One conversation may be enough for the bond to be established. Investigators must know themselves so that psychopaths' attempts at bonding fail. It is valuable for investigators to allow psychopaths to believe they have established rapport with someone inside law enforcement.

Investigators must work as a team, communicate openly, and take all observations seriously. This is necessary for personal self-defense, proficient investigative work, and successful prosecution. Officers must take heed to avoid being impressed with a suspect's credentials and success.

Occasionally, when psychopathic white-collar offenders are identified, they seek out the media and give interviews. They may believe their skills of persuasion are effective enough to convince the public that they have done nothing wrong and are being targeted unjustly by law enforcement. To prevent serious problems with the investigation and prosecution, investigators must remain prepared for all possibilities.

Conclusion

Psychopathy, one of the most studied personality disorders, can cause numerous problems for investigators. Therefore, law enforcement officers must become familiar with psychopaths' traits and characteristics, prevent psychopathic bonds from forming, corroborate information, and take all observations seriously. Investigators must know themselves, work together, communicate with one another openly, and be prepared to deal with the corporate psychopath.

Endnotes

[1] Functional magnetic resonance imaging (FMRI) registers blood flow to functioning areas of the brain.

[2] Hare's Psychopathy Checklist-Revised (PCL-R) is an assessment tool. Psychopathy, as determined by the PCL-R, is indicated by an overall score of 30 or above out of a possible 40. Many point configurations could result in the overall score, determined by adding up the total points for each of the 20 individually listed traits.

[3] Research on psychopathy and lie-detection equipment has yielded conflicting results and remains inconclusive.

[4] Once established that a perpetrator truly is a psychopath, reviewing the videotaped interrogation can be a lesson in their subtle, yet sophisticated manipulation techniques. This is the same method used by psychopathy researchers.

CRITICAL THINKING EXERCISE

In outline form, develop a list of recommendations that could be used for investigators and corporate officers in detecting or interviewing suspected psychopaths. Special attention should be given to predatory and emotionless behaviour—to include violence—violence in the workplace.

ADDRESSING THE PROBLEM OF THE ACTIVE SHOOTER
By Katherine W. Schweit, J.D.

May 2013: *FBI Law Enforcement Bulletin*

UNFORTUNATELY, SCENES INVOLVING ACTIVE SHOOTERS have become too familiar. Radio transmissions of possible shots fired send the closest police officers to the scene. In today's world, such calls carry with them the memories of school, business, and theater shootings.

Responding officers must recognize that more than half of mass-shooting incidents—57 percent—still will be underway, with 75 percent requiring law enforcement personnel to confront the perpetrator before the threat ends.[1] And, one-third of those officers will be shot as they engage.[2]

CRITICAL NEED

That number disturbs FBI Section Chief (SC) Christopher Combs, Strategic Information and Operations Center, the FBI's central command post for all major incidents. He also leads a bureau team assigned by the White House to find ways to support state, local, tribal, and campus law enforcement officers who may face an active-shooter situation. The team's efforts comprise part of a larger initiative, Now Is the Time, begun by the White House after the mass killing of young children at Sandy Hook Elementary School in Newtown, Connecticut.[3]

First responders face the threat of force as part of their daily jobs. Although tactical teams, such as SWAT, train for barricade situations and multiple-member entries, active-shooter training focuses on five-person-or-less building entries. Responding officers may not previously have trained to face this unique type of threat. According to SC Combs, "We've been asked to do our part to help law enforcement better prepare for the next Newtown. With so many officers engaged in shootings, it's important we do whatever we can to help try to change that and make them safer."

IMPORTANT TRAINING

The U.S. Department of Justice (DOJ), Bureau of Justice Assistance (BJA) partially has funded—through its VALOR initiative—the Advanced Law Enforcement Rapid Response Training (ALERRT) course, an active-shooter training program.[4] Born from concerns that arose from shootings at Columbine High School in Littleton, Colorado, ALERRT better prepares the first officers on the scene of an active-shooter situation. The training was developed by the San Marcos, Texas, Police Department and the Hays County, Texas, Sheriff's Department and adopted by Texas State University, San Marcos.

In the aftermath of the tragedy in Sandy Hook, Connecticut, the FBI offered to partner with BJA in the delivery of this crucial training and sent its tactical instructors (TIs) to attend and assess the ALERRT course. The TI program is managed by the Training Division at Quantico, Virginia. As word of training has spread, news of the learning opportunities went national. Since its inception in 2002, ALERRT has trained more than 40,000 law enforcement officers as a result of more than $26 million in funding.

The 16-hour Basic Active-Shooter Course, one of several courses offered, prepares first responders to isolate, distract, and end the threat when an active shooter is engaged. The course covers shooting and moving, conducting threshold evaluations, employing concepts and principles of team movement, using setup and room entry techniques, approaching and breaching the crisis site, practicing rescue-team tactics, handling improvised explosive devices, and recognizing postengagement priorities of work. Training teams carry training-ammunition kits, allowing up to 30 students to engage in tactical force-on-force scenarios carried out in unoccupied schools or office buildings.

Virtually every state has officers trained through the ALERRT program, and many have made the training mandatory for active-shooter responders, the first among them Mississippi, Alabama, Iowa, Louisiana, and South Carolina. Since the Sandy Hook tragedy, more police departments have requested training.

NATIONAL STANDARD, NATIONAL TRAINING
Aware of the increased demand, the FBI agreed to supplement BJA's effort and integrated ALERRT into the White House initiative, reasoning the training could provide added support for law enforcement officers most at risk—those first on the scene. A private study of 35 active-shooter incidents during 2012 found that 37 percent of the attacks ended in less than 5 minutes, 63 percent in less than 15 minutes.[5] Minutes into the Sikh temple shooting in Oak Creek, Wisconsin, the perpetrator turned away from other victims to engage the first officer on the scene and shot him 15 times. Fortunately, the officer survived.[6]

To assist in this project, SC Combs and his team turned to the Tactical Instructors (TIs) in the Law

Enforcement Training for Safety and Survival (LETSS) program, which was developed in 1992. LETSS, a program of the Practical Applications Unit in the FBI's Training Division, strives to provide officers with the skills and mind-set required to identify and handle critical situations in high-risk environments.[7]

LETSS experts recognized the need for coordinated and standardized nationwide active-shooter training and through the FBI/BJA partnership began working directly with ALERRT personnel to study how best to resolve these situations. TIs traveled to the ALERRT center in Texas to observe protocols and ask questions. After working with ALERRT personnel to adjust the course by providing updates and ensuring compliance with current rules and regulations, the FBI adopted the modified course as a national standard.

Since February, 100 FBI TIs have attended the 5-day ALERRT Train-the-Trainer school in San Marcos, Texas. The FBI recognizes that it best serves in a support role as a training partner with BJA. These certified TIs, along with ALERRT instructors, now jointly will be able to provide the 16-hour training at no cost to agencies across the nation. Although funding remains a challenge as federal budget cuts continue, a strong commitment exists to continue to support active-shooter training.

Statistics show that 98 percent of active-shooter incidents involve state and local crimes, primarily occurring in areas with small- and medium-sized law enforcement agencies.[8] Ninety-eight percent of these crimes are carried out by a single shooter, usually male (97 percent).[9]

IMPORTANT DIRECTIVE

On January 14, 2013, President Barack Obama signed the Investigative Assistance for Violent Crimes Act of

2012 into law. The act permits the attorney general, upon the request of an appropriate state or local law enforcement officer, to provide assistance in the investigation of 1) violent acts and shootings occurring in a "place of public use" and 2) mass killings—defined as three or more killings in a single incident—and attempted mass killings. Under the act, federal officials assisting the investigation of these incidents are presumed to be acting within the scope of their employment.

The FBI's efforts include three areas of support. First, before an incident occurs, agencies can obtain no-cost, active-shooter training close to home by submitting a request via the ALERRT website, *http://www.alerrt.org*. The site provides general information, requirements for hosting a school in a particular area, and registration materials. Department officials also can call the special agent in charge of their local FBI field office for further registration assistance.

Second, experts in the FBI's Behavioral Analysis Unit (BAU) are available to conduct threat assessments and develop threat mitigation strategies for persons of concern. BAU is part of the FBI's Critical Incident Response Group, home to the FBI's most sophisticated tactical assets. Each FBI field office has a BAU representative to the FBI's National Center for the Analysis of Violent Crimes (NCAVC). The NCAVC focuses its efforts not on how to respond tactically to an active-shooter situation, but, rather, how to prevent one. These experts can work as part of a team to prevent a situation from escalating by identifying, assessing, and managing the threat.

Third, all FBI field offices are hosting a series of two-day crisis management conferences during 2013 to engage with their state, local, tribal, and campus law enforcement partners and share lessons learned and best practices. The conferences afford attendees an opportunity to share and hear details gleaned from the many after-action reviews the FBI has participated in and observed with involved law enforcement agencies. These provide a plethora of details on how best to deal with unique and complex aspects of these situations, as well as FBI resources available to assist in incident response, management, and resolution.

Conference topics include pre-event and behavioral indicators, evidence collection, complex crime-scene management, strategies to deal with the national news media, procedures for handling IEDs, and methods of providing victim assistance to families and first responders.

Conferences are followed by a newly developed four-hour tabletop exercise for law enforcement agencies and other first responders based on facts relating to the recent school shootings. A second tabletop rolling out in May was specifically designed for college campus incidents. These are designed around the latest lessons learned and best management practices, which will include participation by law enforcement, first responders, fire departments, and other Emergency / public safety agencies.

CONCLUSION

Agencies interested in active-shooter training, conferences, tabletop exercises, or threat-analysis assistance should contact their local FBI office. Doing so may help counter the threat posed by the active shooter. These important educational opportunities may help save civilian lives, as well as the first responders who come to their aid.

ENDNOTES

1 Author follow-on analysis of data from J. Pete Blair and M. Hunter Martaindale, "United States Active Shooter Events from 2000 to 2010: Training and Equipment Implications" (San Marcos, TX: Advanced Law Enforcement Rapid Response Training, Texas State University, 2010), *http://policeforum.org/library/critical-issues-in-policing-series/Blair-UnitedStatesActiveShooterEventsfrom2000to2010Report-Final.pdf* (accessed April 24, 2013).

2 Ibid.

3 White House, "Now is the Time; the President's plan to protect our children and our communities by reducing gun violence," *http://www.whitehouse.gov/issues/preventing-gun-violence* (accessed April 25, 2013).

4 VALOR is a U.S. attorney general initiative that addresses the increase in assaults and violence against law enforcement. For additional information, see *http://www.valorforblue.org/Home.*

5 John Nicoletti, "Detection and Disruption of Insider/Outsider Perpetrated Violence" (lecture, Colorado Emergency Preparedness Partnership, December 2012).

6 Oak Creek Police Department, "After-Action Report, Sikh Temple Shooting, Oak Creek, Wisconsin, August 5, 2012"; Colleen Curry, Michael James, Richard Esposito, and Jack Date, "7 Dead at Sikh Temple in Oak Creek, Wisconsin: Officials Believe 'White Supremacist' Behind 'Domestic Terrorism,'" ABC News, *http://abcnews.go.com/US/sikh-temple-oak-creek-wisconsin-officials-white-supremacist/story?id=16933779#.UXk4xkqyDGo* (accessed April 25, 2013).

7 Federal Bureau of Investigation, "Survival Skills," For additional information, see *http://www.fbi.gov/about-us/training/letts* (accessed April 25, 2013).

8 New York City Police Department, "Active Shooter: Recommendations and Analysis for Risk Mitigation, "*http://www.nyc.gov/html/nypd/downloads/pdf/counterterrorism/ActiveShooter.pdf* (accessed April 24, 2013).

9 Ibid.

10 Ibid.

11 John Nicoletti, "Detection and Disruption of Insider/Outsider Perpetrated Violence."

[12] New York City Police Department, "Active Shooter."
[13] Blair and Martaindale, "United States Active Shooter Events."
[14] Ibid.
[15] Ibid.
[16] Oak Creek Police Department; Lieutenant Paul Vance.
[17] Blair and Martaindale, "United States Active Shooter Events."
[18] Ibid.

DISCUSSION QUESTION

Do you think that law-enforcement agencies in your local community (campus or municipal) have obtained the FBI training for active shooters as described in this article?

CRITICAL THINKING EXERCISE

If you were developing a comprehensive "active-shooter" training program for a borough or campus law enforcement agency, what do you think the elements of the training program should include? Make sure to reference violence risk assessment, needs assessment, critical training components, and methods of maintaining perishable skills.

ABDUCTION BY VEHICULAR ASSAULT

By

James O. Beasley II, M.P.A., and

Jennifer D. Eakin, M.A.

November 2012: *FBI Law Enforcement Bulletin*

ON A LONELY HIGHWAY IN A RURAL AREA, A TEENAGE BOY makes his way down the road, turning to show his thumb to the occasional passing vehicle. He hears an approaching vehicle behind him as it slows down, and he begins to turn around in hopes of finally getting a ride. He feels a sudden, painful impact as he is struck and propelled through the air, landing in a nearby ditch. Stunned and bleeding, he hears approaching footsteps and is lifted into the backseat of the vehicle as the driver starts the car and continues down the road. Just as suddenly, he realizes that his rescuer has pulled off the road again and also has entered the backseat.

As the boy lapses in and out of consciousness, he feels a man's hands on his body. Sometime later the victim is revived by the coolness of the night air as he is pulled from the car and thrown to the ground. He hears the slamming of the car door, the diminishing drone of the engine, and then nothing more.

This scenario describes a previously unrecognized form of blitz-style attack where a vehicle is used to quickly overpower and capture a victim. An offender with a history of blitz-style assaults makes initial physical contact from the safe confines of a vehicle, which serves as both a weapon and a means of transporting the victim to another location, generally to commit a sexual assault.

For this article, the term *blitz* is defined as the rapid application of overwhelming physical force intended to injure, incapacitate, or gain control of a victim.[1] The forceful approach of blitz-style offenders represents a predominant strategy, not an aberration. The cases discussed in this article illustrate that when an unknown offender is responsible for an otherwise puzzling series of blitz-style assaults, the individual sometimes also may resort to a variation of the familiar blitz theme by using an automobile to obtain a victim. Recognizing this connection and understanding the behavioral and personality characteristics associated with blitz-style offenders may allow investigators to develop additional leads.

While it is not standard practice in a serial murder case to review all reports of vehicle-on-pedestrian (VOP) collisions, investigators, nevertheless, should consider this strategy for crimes that involve blitz assaults.[2]

FIRST CASE
A serial child abductor who sexually assaulted and murdered three victims—all males from 12 to 15 years of age—admitted his involvement in the murders to a cellmate while incarcerated for burglary, which was his only prior conviction. All criminal acts attributed to the offender occurred within a 100-mile radius over a 4-year period and began when he was 21 years old. A review of the investigative reports in combination with

the offender's account revealed his predominantly blitz-style approach toward victims. Though the significance of this approach was not recognized at the time, it later was noted that the offender had a driving history that included at least two hit-and-run incidents. In reality, both were attempts to capture victims—who were strangers to the offender—using a vehicle to stun or disable.

In his daily existence and while committing his crimes, the offender consistently demonstrated limited social skills. A school psychologist described him as immature and having a low self-image. His IQ was measured as 91, considered low-average. He held menial jobs, continued to live with his parents into adulthood, and was notably deficient in his problem-solving abilities.

For example, the solution to his perceived problem of having a small penis was to inject it with cooking grease in an effort to enlarge it. An emergency room visit with a short period of hospitalization occurred as a result. Additionally, when describing the moment in which a murder occurred, he invariably ended with the statement "and then batteries out" in reference to a victim's death. The obvious limitations in his ability to effectively communicate may have prompted the offender to resort to the use of an automobile to solve the problem of obtaining a desired victim without the awkward and, ultimately, futile attempt to interact.

Crimes
First Murder (1981)
The offender was acquainted with the family of his first victim and was a regular visitor to their home, located a few blocks from his own residence. He entered the victim's dwelling uninvited late one night and, according to his statement, lured the 15-year-old boy with the promise of alcohol. The victim left his home

without shoes, a jacket, or a wallet, bringing into question the voluntariness of his departure. Driving his own vehicle, the offender took the boy to a secluded area 7 to 8 miles away where he immediately began a violent assault that included manually strangling the victim, slashing the boy's throat with a knife, and striking him repeatedly on the head with a rock. The sudden and continued onslaught soon led to the victim's death, after which the offender admitted to performing postmortem sexual acts on the body. When the boy's family discovered him missing the next morning, the local community, including the offender, joined them in the search for the missing victim. His body remained undiscovered for 5 years.

Second Murder (1984)
The offender confronted a 12-year-old boy on a trail near the victim's junior high school and asked for the time. Though he was a stranger, the boy responded and turned away. The offender then grabbed him from behind and put a knife to his throat. When the victim struggled, the perpetrator stabbed him 23 times and moved his body into some nearby bushes, where it was discovered approximately 3 hours later. When questioned about the incident, the offender acknowledged observing the victim's penis, although he denied any direct sexual contact.

Third Murder (1985)
The offender was riding his bicycle on a well-known trail one evening when he spotted a 12-year-old boy, also a stranger, riding a bicycle. He pursued the victim down the trail, bumping the boy's bike with his own as the victim attempted to ride away. The offender then pulled both bikes and the boy into some nearby bushes and ordered him to undress. He immediately assaulted the victim with an ice pick, stabbing him twice in the chest. By the offender's account, he lay on top of the victim, kissed him on the mouth, and inserted the ice pick into the victim's eye near the tear

duct, which the offender described as reminding him of anal intercourse. The body was discovered 6 days later.

Driving History

In August 1982 while traveling at 40 mph in his vehicle, the offender struck a 17-year-old male from the rear who was on a moped. The perpetrator dragged the victim and moped, which had become entangled in the vehicle, approximately 30 feet, then turned off his headlights, backed up, and fled the scene. The boy observed the license plate, which he provided to authorities, resulting in the offender's arrest for misdemeanor hit-and-run. In October 1982 the offender pled guilty and was fined $150. Authorities never recognized this incident as an attempted abduction, although during a later interview the offender described it as exactly that. He admitted leaving the scene without completing the abduction because the victim was not sufficiently incapacitated by the collision.

A similar incident occurred 3 months later when the offender, who was driving a vehicle, struck a 16-year-old male walking home from a party, severely injuring the boy with the impact. The offender put the incapacitated victim into his vehicle and drove to a remote area where he dumped the victim down a steep ravine and left him for dead. The boy's injuries included a lacerated spleen, a ruptured bladder, multiple pelvic fractures, and a concussion. Though the boy survived, the case remained unsolved for the next 4 years. It officially was characterized as a hit-and-run and was not recognized as an attempted abduction. By the offender's account, he did not intend to "damage" the victim as badly as he did; he meant, instead, to disable the boy to facilitate his abduction. As typical of this offender, he denied sexually molesting the unconscious victim.

In the context of the offender's overall criminal conduct during the 3-year period between the first and second murders, his driving history assumes greater significance. Although the two vehicular incidents in 1982 both resulted in physical injury to young men, neither was recognized at the time as an unsuccessful abduction attempt. This is an example of a serial killer who continued to act out criminally through conduct not generally associated with his other criminal acts. However, his practice of blitzing victims with an automobile is essentially consistent with that behavior. More important, the personality characteristics of offenders who choose this strategy may have more in common than previously recognized.

SECOND CASE

An offender committed four blitz-style assaults at age 18 against white females between the ages of 24 and 49. All of the attacks were sexually motivated, with one of them resulting in a completed rape and homicide. These offenses occurred within a 10-month period and were confined to a 5-mile radius in two adjoining communities. The victims all were strangers to the offender and were confronted and assaulted outdoors at or near their homes. The perpetrator brought and used a weapon in each assault, which was initiated without any preliminary verbal engagement. At the time of his arrest, he had only one prior felony conviction for a burglary that occurred amidst the series of assaults.

A sense of the offender's everyday interactions can be gleaned from school records and interpersonal relationships. For instance, he was expelled from high school for behavioral issues and was referred to an alternative education program, which he also failed to complete. He developed an alcohol and drug problem during this time frame, but it is unknown whether this was related to his poor academic performance. He held menial jobs and had at least two girlfriends in late adolescence. Although there were no accounts of him acting out violently in the context of those relationships, reports indicated that he had a violent streak and a volatile temper. For instance, during a disagreement with someone considered to be a close friend, he head-butted the young man and broke his nose. Additionally, he was described as "smart and calculating," reportedly excelling during a chess competition against the Princeton University Chess Club at the prison where he was incarcerated. When characterizing his own criminal conduct in a postarrest interview, he indicated experiencing powerful and irresistible urges prior to the assaults.

Crimes

First Assault (February 2003)
While on foot, the offender approached a 37-year-old female from behind while she was removing items from her vehicle in her driveway and talking on a cell phone. He grabbed her arm and, brandishing a box cutter, attempted to drag her away from the residence. The only words he uttered during the assault were "come on, come on." Punches were exchanged during the struggle, allowing the victim to break free and scream while running toward home. Her husband ran out of the house and gave chase, but the offender escaped. Due to his hasty retreat and with no indication of motive at the scene, it was only through the offender's later statement that authorities could infer a sexual motivation.[3]

Second Assault (March 2003)
A 49-year-old female was walking on the road near her residence when the offender, who was walking in the opposite direction, reversed course and came at her from behind, hitting her in the head repeatedly with a tire iron and causing her to fall to the ground. The offender straddled her legs, unbuttoned her pants, and

began to remove them with both hands, putting down the weapon in the process. When the victim attempted to pick up the weapon, the offender aborted the assault, retrieved the tire iron, and fled into a nearby neighborhood. He took cash from the woman while leaving her jewelry untouched. Throughout the assault, the offender remained silent. According to detectives, the tire iron, still bearing the victim's blood, was recovered from the offender's vehicle when he was arrested over a year later. The woman received 16 stitches to her head and sustained damage to her hand, which required multiple surgeries.

Third Assault/Homicide (May 2003)
A 24-year-old female was returning to her residence late one night when she was attacked at her front door by the offender, who stabbed her repeatedly with a knife. A blood trail led from her townhome down the sidewalk and ended two doors away in a clump of bushes where she was found. The victim died in the hospital 2 days after the assault. There were a total of 19 stab wounds, and both her pants and panties were pulled down.

Though the woman could not describe the details of her attack, all indications were consistent with a blitz-style assault. When later interviewed, the perpetrator described the immediate violence of the assault, as well as his persistence once it was initiated; he also spoke of briefly hiding nearby after the attack to ensure that no one had been alerted by the victim's screams. When he returned to complete the sexual assault, the offender believed the woman "was dying, unconscious," which he inferred from her labored breathing.

Fourth Assault (November 2003)
The offender initially walked past the victim, a 45-year-old female, while casually smoking a cigarette before turning and immediately beginning his attack.

He grabbed her from behind and while wielding a knife began to stab her in the head, neck, face, and chest, continuing the assault as she fell to the ground. According to the victim, who survived, the offender never spoke to her and abruptly broke off his assault and left the scene. Police reports indicated the woman's pants were unbuttoned when they arrived. Although she did not describe the assault as sexually motivated, a subsequent interview with the offender revealed his sexual intent.

The perpetrator came to the attention of authorities through witnesses who noted his similarity to a composite drawing, which police had circulated. A list of look-alikes was whittled down through interviewing, collecting and verifying alibi information, and requesting a DNA sample.[4] From a cigarette butt and fingernail scrapings, DNA recovered at the scene of the fourth assault linked the offender to the attack and, ultimately, to the homicide 6 months prior. When asked to describe his thoughts at the time of the homicide, he stated, "They felt like sexual impulses...I just felt the impulses...I don't know." This apparent lack of insight and inability to articulate his motivation is common among blitz-style offenders.

Driving History
Following his arrest in 2004, the offender not only confessed to the assaults and the homicide but also admitted that a prior traffic incident was a failed attempt to obtain another victim. The incident— occurring in August 2003 between the third and fourth assaults—involved the perpetrator in a vehicle crossing the opposing lane of traffic and hitting a female jogger from behind. He later admitted he intentionally struck her with the objective of getting her into the vehicle and committing another sexual assault. He did not circle the block to come back for the woman; on his admission, "I hit her with the car. I rammed into her

. . . and I just went vroom."

When a potential witness appeared after calling 911, the subject aborted his plan to abduct and told the responding officer that he had become distracted when he dropped a lit cigarette in his lap. The victim challenged his account, claiming she heard his engine rev just prior to being struck, but the offender was only cited for careless driving, an infraction that did not result in a loss of driving privileges. The victim, who was catapulted over the hood of the vehicle, was taken to a local hospital where she was treated for multiple abrasions and later released.

It is not surprising that the individual responsible for this series of blitz-style assaults using a knife, tire iron, and his fists also was involved in a driving incident in which the quality of the assault was similar except that a vehicle was used in place of a more traditional weapon. Therefore, it may be necessary to expand the concept of blitz-style offenders to include, on some occasions, the use of a weapon on four wheels.

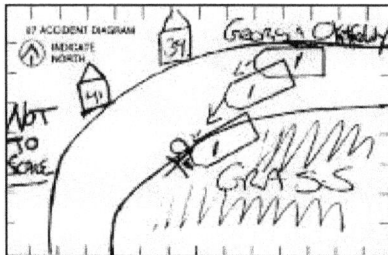

Sketch from the accident report of an attempted abduction using vehicular blitz. The offender was cited for careless driving and released.

VEHICULAR ASSAULT VS. HIT-AND-RUN

Admittedly, most hit-and-run incidents are not attempts by offenders to obtain victims for potential abductions. Hit-and-runs often occur as a result of driver impairment due to drug or alcohol use, dementia, drowsiness, or distraction.[5] The decision to run may be due to emotional factors, such as fear, panic, or confusion, often compounded by the impairment.

There are two active components implied in a hit-and-run. The first involves physical contact and a presumed awareness of that contact by the driver. The second entails a decision to leave or flee the scene. The awareness component may be the most problematic aspect of proving a hit-and-run case. Examples in the news media depict drivers who do not realize they hit someone or believe they hit an animal, rather than a person. Their alleged lack of awareness may confound investigations into the events, especially if they are not witnessed by a third party. Consequently, many hit-and-run cases result in lesser charges, such as reckless driving, unsafe operation of a motor vehicle, speeding, and failure to yield.

Police statistics alone may not reveal how many VOP incidents occur in a given year. For example, a 2005 study in San Francisco, California, found that 21 percent of all VOP traffic accidents were not reported to the police.[6] This was evidenced by a discrepancy between hospital records documenting treatment of individuals for injuries sustained during such collisions and police reports filed on those incidents. In other words, some victims seeking medical attention after being struck by vehicles did not file corresponding police reports. Although it cannot be quantified, a small number of those collisions may have been failed abduction attempts.

When a vehicle comes into contact with a body, the degree of physical injury can be significant, even at fairly low speeds. For instance, if a person is hit by a vehicle traveling at 14 miles per hour, the legs begin to fracture. At 45 miles per hour, amputation of limbs may occur. At 55 miles per hour, amputation or transection of the body almost is certain.[7]

Most drivers are inexperienced with the real consequences of VOP accidents and, therefore, lack a full understanding of the potential devastation of striking a person with a vehicle. Even an individual who, in fact, is attempting to obtain a victim is relying on guesswork to estimate the logistics of hitting the victim. An offender easily could misjudge the amount of force needed to accomplish the capture. If underestimated, the victim could be slightly injured but still able to flee, resist, and report the incident. If overestimated, the victim could be killed or injured so severely that they no longer are appealing to the offender.

The first few minutes after an offender attempts to capture a victim are the riskiest. The perpetrator may feign innocence, appearing to offer assistance while closing the gap between predator and prey but still preserving plausible deniability. If interrupted while placing the victim into the vehicle, the offender can choose to abort the abduction and explain that they only were preparing to transport the victim to the hospital.

Offenders may be able to reduce their legal exposure from an attempted abduction to a traffic citation if they do not panic. However, as previously described, their level of social and cognitive functioning may range on the continuum but often tends toward the lower end of the spectrum. Therefore, all blitz-style offenders may not be equally resourceful in offering a believable explanation to authorities.

Interview Example

In the following excerpt from a research interview conducted by members of the FBI's Behavioral Analysis Unit, the offender described the application of a blitz approach utilizing

> *Inmate:* "I rode up, and he had kind of stopped to let me go by, and I kind of tapped him just slightly, and once I had tapped his bike, that gave me a reason to get out, so he wouldn't freak out while I was getting out of the truck, and I got out and walked around, and I said, 'Hey, are you OK?' and I just kind of picked him up and sat him in the truck."

> *Interviewer:* "That's a pretty impulsive thing to do and pretty risky."

> *Inmate:* "Yeah, I never said I was a criminal genius."

For background, the victim in this case was knocked to the ground and temporarily stunned by the collision, thereby facilitating his speedy removal from the scene. The primary motivation was sexual, and an assault occurred soon after the abduction. The victim survived and was eventually rescued.

Blitz-Offender Traits

This article describes in detail numerous crimes committed by two blitz-style offenders who, it later was learned, also used an automobile as a weapon in attempting to subdue and capture victims. Individuals who repeatedly commit blitz-style assaults and use their vehicles as a variation of that method demonstrate similar mechanics in the commission of their crimes and possess some common behavioral and personality traits.

- The victims are usually strangers and often female. Selection may be based more on availability and vulnerability than physical appearance.

- The motive is sexual, although the sexual aspect of the assaults—nontraditional or, even, postmortem sexual behavior—may not be readily apparent, perhaps, due to lack of time or planning.

- Little or no verbal interaction occurs with victims prior to or during the attack.

- Crimes are need-driven rather than thought-driven and, therefore, may occur in high-risk circumstances, such as in broad daylight or with witnesses in the area.

- A handheld weapon often is used in assaults not involving a vehicle.

- Little or no planning or preparation is done. As a result, offenders' crimes may not go well or may be aborted or modified abruptly. This can result in a crime scene that is hard to interpret because the objective was not achieved.

- Items of value may be undisturbed or overlooked, possibly because the primary objective is sexual. If items are taken, it is usually done as an afterthought.

- Little consideration is given to body disposal if the attack results in a homicide. Therefore, victims usually are found quickly.

- An irresistible urge to strike out overcomes offenders. The origins or possible precipitating circumstances for this often are unknown.

- Social or communication deficits are present and often noted early in their histories. School records also may reflect learning or developmental disabilities, which further may impede their ability to interact in mainstream society.[8]

- Interpersonal relationships include incidents of violent outbursts without apparent provocation and seemingly out of proportion to the offense.

- Financial or emotional dependency on family members is present and often extends into adulthood. This makes it less likely that these individuals will leave the area where family resides.

- They often are perceived as loners, even within a household, because of their social isolation, which may breed suspicion and paranoia on their part concerning the intentions of others.

- Criminal history is evident by their early 20s (sometimes with an extant juvenile record) relating to drugs, impulsivity, and antisocial behavior.

- Anecdotal or documented drug abuse, including alcohol, exists from their early years.

Possible Investigative Strategies
The use of a vehicle as a weapon is not a new concept. There are numerous accounts of individuals who deliberately run down an errant spouse or strike an officer while attempting to avoid apprehension. However, the phenomenon described in this article is radically different from those examples. The motive in this type of blitz attack instead is aimed at obtaining a victim. While unsophisticated and even primitive as a

technique, it can be more challenging to recognize because it defies the expectations of law enforcement. When faced with a series of unsolved blitz attacks in which a vehicle was used, two possible investigative strategies can help bring about answers.

1) When a series of blitz-style assaults is attributed to a single offender, investigators should consider reviewing driving histories to identify local individuals with hit-and-run records and related traffic offenses. Any incident details, including references to a collision or near collision with a pedestrian or cyclist, should be selected for closer review. Local emergency room records for treatment of injuries commonly associated with hit-and-run accidents also warrant review due to the underreporting of such incidents.

2) Officers investigating crime scenes involving VOP collisions should consider the possibility that the offense may have been an attempt by the driver to obtain a victim. Under normal conditions most hit-and-run incidents involve either a pedestrian who was at fault or a driver who somehow was impaired. While the use of a motor vehicle to gain control of a victim is a rare occurrence, when it does happen, it often is overlooked or mischaracterized during an investigation.

CONCLUSION
In many cases it may be relatively easy to recognize the work of a blitz-style offender, particularly when the manifestation meets expectations of what a blitz assault should entail. Thorough examination of the crime scene, paired with a report from a surviving victim, can readily confirm that a blitz assault has occurred. Based on the discussion and analysis in this article, avenues of investigation, such as these, can supply law enforcement with the necessary knowledge to more effectively address the criminal behaviors of

blitz-style offenders.

Endnotes

[1] Ann W. Burgess, Robert A. Prentky, and Elizabeth B. Dowdell, "Sexual Predators in Nursing Homes," in *Practical Aspects of Rape Investigation: A Multidisciplinary Approach*, 3rd ed., ed. Robert R. Hazelwood and Ann W. Burgess (Boca Raton, FL: CRC Press, 2001), 489-490; John Douglas, Ann W. Burgess, Allen G. Burgess, and Robert K. Ressler, *Crime Classification Manual: A Standard System for Investigating and Classifying Violent Crimes*, 1st ed. (New York, NY: Lexington Books, 1992), 351; Brent E. Turvey, ed., *Criminal Profiling: An Introduction to Behavioral Evidence Analysis*, 1st ed. (London, UK: Academic Press, 1999), 125-127; and Jisun Park, Louis B. Schlesinger, Anthony J. Pinizzotto, Edward F. Davis, "Serial and Single-Victim Rapists: Differences in Crime-Scene Violence, Interpersonal Involvement, and Criminal Sophistication," *Behavioral Sciences and the Law* 26, no. 2 (March/April 2008): 227-237.

[2] The VOP label also includes cyclists and operators of scooter-type conveyances.

[3] The crude and poorly planned nature of this attack by such a skilled chess player is instructive to investigators, indicating that intelligent criminals do not necessarily commit intelligent crimes.

[4] In similar cases, an offender's willingness to provide DNA has sometimes led investigators to eliminate them as a suspect without taking a sample. It often is assumed that no guilty person would voluntarily hand over evidence that would convict them.

[5] "Why Drivers Hit and Run?" Hit and Run Accidents on America's Deadly Roads, entry posted May 2003, *http://www.deadlyroads.com/whydriversrun.shtml* (accessed June 26, 2013).

[6] Stanley Sciortino, Mary Vassar, Michael Radetsky, and M. Margaret Knudson, "San Francisco Pedestrian Injury Surveillance: Mapping, Underreporting, and Injury Severity in Police and Hospital Records," *Accident Analysis and Prevention* 37, no. 6 (November 2005): 1102-1113.

[7] Stan Oglesby, Midwest Accident Reconstruction Services, L.C., personal communication with authors, January 2007.

[8] Social deficits are more important than IQ in describing these offenders. Although cognitive ability may impact social development, one can have a higher IQ and still be socially marginal.

DISCUSSION QUESTION

Compare and contrast the *blitz* attack described in this article with the rape typology of the same name.

CRITICAL THINKING EXERCISE

When providing security risk and threat assessments, the criminal element should always be taken into consideration. In other words, the threats are not posed solely by elements of organized crime or foreign intelligence services, but also by ordinary criminals or rapists and killers as described in this article. Accordingly, your assignment is to develop some guidelines on how to brief clients for awareness purposes relative to attacks of this sort.

"Crisis" or "Hostage" Negotiation?
The Distinction Between Two Important Terms

By Jeff Thompson

March 2014: *FBI Law Enforcement Bulletin*

CRISIS NEGOTIATION HAS BEEN DESCRIBED AS BEING ONE of law enforcement's most effective tools. As we celebrate the anniversary of the world-renowned Hostage Negotiation Team (HNT) that was created in 1973 by the New York City Police Department (NYPD), it is worth taking a look at the use of the words "crisis" and "hostage."

The NYPD's HNT was the first-ever unit created to deal specifically in negotiating with individuals involved in a crisis and possible hostage situation. To this day, they are looked upon as one of the best in the world. Prior to the creation of the HNT, the standard police response to these situations was to tell the person to surrender immediately—if the individual did not comply, police personnel would lay siege in an attempt to resolve the situation.

This method of response contributed to the people involved (including the hostage taker, the hostages and victims, police, and bystanders) being injured and sometimes killed in various incidents. The HNT provided what is common in conflict resolution practices—an alternative method based on communication skills and collaboration.

As time has passed since the NYPD's HNT was created, something noticeable has occurred in the realm of law enforcement hostage negotiation—the emergence of the word "crisis" being used and often replacing the term "hostage." Reviewing academic literature, one will find the term "crisis negotiation" being commonly accepted while television and other media outlets still refer to "hostage" as the generalized term.[1]

The Federal Bureau of Investigation's (FBI) Crisis Negotiation Unit (CNU) is arguably the most well-known negotiation unit due to, among many other reasons, the professional and comprehensive training they provide to their special agents and law enforcement agencies across the country, as well as to foreign police personnel. The FBI's unit however does not have the word "hostage" in its name.

Are the words "crisis" and "hostage" interchangeable? Is there a difference between the two? If so, which is the correct word? The quick answers are no, yes, and it depends.

Incidents involving law enforcement negotiators

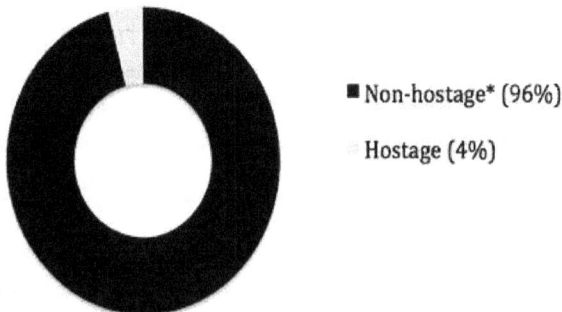

■ Non-hostage* (96%)

Hostage (4%)

* Non-hostage incidents include barricaded subjects with or without victims, and suicidal subjects. Source: FBI HOBAS. Report generated August 22, 2013.

According to the Hostage Barricade Database System (HOBAS)—a database containing information about barricade incidents maintained by the FBI's CNU—96 percent of incidents requiring the response of law enforcement do not include a hostage being taken. That means only 4 percent of these situations involved a person taking another person or persons hostage. The infographic in Table 1 has additional hostage and crisis negotiator data provided by HOBAS.

A hostage is a person taken involuntarily and being held by the perpetrator with plans to trade them for something else in return. This can include a mode of transportation with plans to escape, money, release of prisoners, or items such as food and drinks.

What is it then when a person is being held against their will yet the situation does not fit the above example? Both situations would be considered a "crisis," yet in the second situation, the person that is being held involuntarily would not be called a "hostage" but rather a "victim." Therefore, a hostage situation is one type of crisis to which law enforcement negotiators will respond.

Looking at the statistics, if only 4 percent of incidents involve a hostage situation, what do the rest entail? Included in the remaining 96 percent are emotionally-driven crises where a person is barricaded by themselves or with one or more victims, or is suicidal. In these situations, the person is not making substantive demands or asking for anything from the police because they do not need anything from the police. Rather, they are in crisis, meaning that their normal coping mechanisms for dealing with life's day-to-day challenges have been overwhelmed. Their emotion level is high while their rational ability is low.

Table 2

Law Enforcement Association Names			
Use "hostage" (9)	**Use "crisis" (8)**	**Use both (1)**	**Use neither (2)**
Baltimore County Hostage Negotiation Team	Arizona Crisis Negotiation Team	Indiana Assoc. of Hostage-Crisis Negotiators	Delaware Valley Negotiators Assoc.
California Assoc. of Hostage Negotiators	Crisis Negotiators Assoc. of Wisconsin		Northern Ohio Negotiators Assoc.
Florida Assoc. of Hostage Negotiators	New England Crisis Negotiators Assoc.		
Kansas Assoc. of Hostage Negotiators	Illinois Crisis Negotiators Assoc.		
Michigan Association of Hostage Negotiators	Louisiana Assoc. of Crisis Negotiators		
New York Assoc. of Hostage Negotiators	Midwest Crisis Negotiators		
Rocky Mountain Association of Hostage Negotiators	South Carolina Crisis Negotiators Association		
Texas Association of Hostage Negotiators	(Washington) Crisis Negotiations Work Group		
Western States Hostage Negotiation Assoc.			

While reviewing the names of police associations related to hostage and crisis negotiators, there is not a clear preference with respect to using "crisis" or "hostage" in a given name. Table 2 details this while also showing two cases in which neither is used and one in which both are used.

It is not the suggestion of this author that units or associations should be using the word "crisis" based on the HOBAS statistics—rather, this article has set out to explain the distinction between the two terms. Is this distinction worth considering when deciding which word to use? The choice is yours—at the very least you are informed.

DISCUSSION QUESTIONS

1. What do you think? Does it make any difference as to which word is used, crisis or hostage?

2. Do you agree with the author's claim that the Federal Bureau of Investigation's (FBI) Crisis Negotiation Unit (CNU) is arguably the most well-known negotiation unit due to, among many other reasons, the professional and comprehensive training they provide to their special agents and law enforcement agencies across the country, as well as to foreign police personnel? Compare the frequency of their work to hostage negotiators with NYPD and LAPD.

DIVERSION SAFES

By Megan C. Bolduc, M.A., M.S.

April 2012: *FBI Law Enforcement Bulletin*

URING INVESTIGATIONS AND OTHER DAILY OPERATIONS, law enforcement personnel frequently conduct extensive searches of individuals' residences, offices, and other personal spaces when authorized by law. As a result, criminals strive to conceal illegal items in case of such a search, and they may hide this material inside containers known as "diversion safes."

Manufacturers advertise diversion safes for their legal purpose—as a way to protect one's valuables. However, diversion safes disguised as common household items also can provide criminals a convenient hiding place for incriminating items, such as narcotics, weapons, and cash. The Naval Criminal Investigative Service (NCIS) first reported on diversion safes in 1997, and the product lines have expanded even further since that time.

Law enforcement personnel must remain aware of the variety of safes available and the wide array of Internet and retail stores that sell them. This knowledge can help investigators identify the containers and, thus, discover illegal material that otherwise might have passed undetected through a routine search. Law enforcement personnel must become educated about the popularity of this diversion technique, the types and characteristics of available products, and the possible impact on officers' efforts.

Availability

Diversion safe product lines have expanded significantly in recent years, and the number of Internet and retail outlets that sell these products also has increased. Both of these factors make it easier than ever for individuals to purchase the safes and, potentially, thwart investigations. Diversion safes are widely available from popular online retailers and in local home goods stores. They also are affordable, with prices ranging from just a few dollars up to $40.

Characteristics

Many diversion safes can appear as common household items. For example, weapons can be hidden in mantle clocks, drugs can be stowed cleverly in what appears to be a soda bottle, and money can fit inside of all sorts of canisters. Because these items are not common hiding places that officers search routinely, the illicit materials inside the safes may remain undetected.

Such safes are crafted to look and feel exactly like the products that they mimic. They also are weighted to feel like a normal object, so even if officers hold a safe, they will not discover the contents inside unless they examine the item closely and remove the top or bottom. Diversion safes come in many shapes and sizes and may be disguised as personal care products, household items, food, or beverages.

Many safes are exact replicas of the items they mimic because they are remanufactured from the original containers. For example, a soda can safe may be advertised as a realistic replica that feels full of liquid, does not open accidentally, and has a top that must be screwed on and off to access the inside. A water bottle safe may include real water, with the bottom filled with liquid and with a hidden area behind the label. Candle diversion safes may function as real candles and burn for up to 4 hours, which largely decreases suspicion of the item's actual purpose.

Legitimate Functions

Any individual could purchase a diversion safe for a legitimate purpose (e.g., to thwart potential thieves and conceal valuable possessions). As such, most safe manufacturers advertise their products as a repository for legal materials, such as jewelry or cash. Manufacturers named these containers diversion safes for this reason—they divert the attention of thieves and allow individuals to hide their valuables in plain sight. Manufacturers promote the safes' effectiveness in preventing theft because criminals often are in a hurry and, therefore, likely will grab only the most visible valuables. Product descriptions may claim the containers hide anything the owner does not want found in the home, office, car, or dorm.

Nefarious Use

While diversion safes can serve a legitimate purpose for many customers, they also may attract the attention of criminals. Just as these products can fool thieves, they can divert police officers during a search, and dangerous items easily can be concealed in these containers. Because the manufacturers advertise that these products can hold anything people need to conceal, this suggests they can hide items, such as weapons and illegal narcotics, that if discovered would incriminate criminals.

Drugs are popular items to hide. To this end, retailers may advertise the safes as a place to conceal legally prescribed drugs from thieves. While such advertisements may not discuss criminal activity, a product advertised as a discreet repository for drugs may garner interest from illegal narcotics users.

Manufacturers have created diversion safes to hide pills in small items, such as skateboard wheels, car cigarette lighters, and batteries. A pen diversion safe, available for only a few dollars, can hide money and prescription drugs discreetly while working as a fully functional pen. When the top unscrews, the pen reveals a hidden compartment and removable vial.

The illicit functions of diversion safes became more publicized in 2007 when a professional football player was suspected of attempting to smuggle marijuana through airport security. He arrived at the airport carrying a 20-ounce water bottle, which security personnel told him he could not carry to his gate. When Transportation Security Administration (TSA) screeners inspected the bottle more closely, they discovered that it actually was a diversion safe with a hidden compartment containing what apparently was marijuana. The compartment remained hidden by the bottle's label so that it appeared to be a full bottle of water when held upright.[1]

Concealment in Vehicles

Diversion safes in vehicles pose additional risks for law enforcement. Because officers commonly discover incriminating items during roadside searches, many individuals hide drugs and other illegal items in their cars. To this end, diversion safes have become a popular method of concealment.

Many companies sell containers specifically created for vehicles, such as a safe that resembles a can of tire sealant or a thermal coffee mug. Because drivers commonly keep such products in a car, they do not draw officers' attention during a search. These safes make it easier for criminals to transport illegal items in their vehicles without suspicion.

Implications for Law Enforcement

Many law enforcement duties involve searches of homes, offices, and vehicles. Diversion safes present an attractive option for criminals to keep their illegal items out of an officer's sight, even during a search. Therefore, these safes can cause serious problems for law enforcement personnel if potential evidence remains concealed in what appear to be ordinary objects.

Diversion safes' rising popularity and availability should cause officers even greater concern and motivate them to take extra care when they search suspects' personal property. The fact that these safes look and feel exactly like the items they mimic, even if examined, makes them especially difficult for officers to spot. As such, officers may need to spend additional time when conducting searches to ensure that they thoroughly inspect all possible hiding places.

Because safe manufacturers advertise their products as a theft-prevention method, marketing materials may claim that law enforcement personnel endorse the products. They might even advertise that officers encourage homeowners to buy the safes.

Homemade Versions

Many Web sites post written instructions and videos to teach users how to make secret compartments out of household items, such as decks of cards, CD cases, mp3 players, and travel coffee cups. These instructional materials increase the availability and accessibility of safes, especially for juveniles. If individuals can make their own safes, they no longer have to spend money to purchase them or wait for them to be delivered. Such how-to videos teach criminals to cheaply and effectively hide items that may be of interest to law enforcement, particularly if they expect to undergo a search of their belongings and property.

Parental Concerns

Diversion safes also may attract juveniles who want to hide illegal items from their parents. To combat this, the Prevent Delinquency Project teaches parents strategies to spot diversion safes in their homes.[2] The Web site informs parents about popular concealment tactics, such as the use of hollowed-out books, soda cans, and deodorant containers with secret compartments or false bottoms. Also, it warns that more recently, acquiring such items has become even easier for juveniles.[3]

The site provides valuable information on trends and news related to diversion safes to help educate parents; this same information can prove useful for law enforcement personnel. For example, the site discusses "stash" water bottles sold on the Internet and warns that parents often overlook them because the top and bottom sections of the bottles contain water. If parents and law enforcement personnel are aware of these creative tactics, they more successfully can prevent children from possessing dangerous items.

Conclusion

Undoubtedly, many people desire to conceal their possessions for any number of reasons. These instances can include teenagers hiding alcohol from their parents, homeowners safeguarding jewelry from potential thieves, or drug users storing marijuana in their vehicles. Diversion safes provide an attractive method of concealment for all of these groups. As such, the potential for the use of the safes is high. The vast array of companies and stores that offer these products, in addition to the large quantity and variety of safes available, demonstrates their popularity.

Despite their possible lawful functions, diversion safes in the hands of criminals can cause serious problems for law enforcement. Diversion safes can conceal contraband in homes, offices, vehicles, luggage, and other areas subject to search. If officers are not aware of these items, they may allow illicit materials to pass through a search undetected. Because these safes so closely resemble the items they mimic, officers must remain alert for common items that contain secret compartments. This may require longer and more comprehensive searches to ensure the officers examine all potential hiding places. Through increased awareness of this diversion technique, officers can identify criminal activity and uncover items of evidentiary value.

Endnotes

[1] B.N. Sullivan, "NFL Quarterback's Fake Water Bottle Intercepted at MIA," *http://aircrewbuzz.com/2007/01/nfl-quarterbacks-fake-water-bottle.html*(accessed December 1, 2010).

[2] *http://www.preventdelinquency.org* (accessed February 14, 2012).

[3] *http://www.preventdelinquency.org/child-threat-drugs.php* (accessed December 14, 2010).

Critical Thinking Exercise

Undertake a search of the Internet to see the various types of "diversion" safes that are available on the market. Describe the different types and how they can be used to conceal evidence or contraband in homes or motor vehicles. Offer advice on how to recognize these items for what they are so as to distinguish them from other, non-diversionary objects, if possible.

KIDNAPPING CASE VIGNETTES

Reprinted From:

U.S. Army TRADOC G2
Kidnapping and Terror
In the Contemporary Operational Environment

When we hijack a plane it has more effect than if we kill a hundred...in battle...For decades, world opinion has been neither for nor against the Palestinians. It simply ignored us. At least the world is talking about us now.
George Habash
Interview in German magazine *Der Stern* in 1970

THIS CHAPTER PROVIDES EXAMPLES OF KIDNAPPING incident analysis and implications. A methodology model of case study introduces basic principles to guide case development such as abstract, introduction, learning objectives, and case overview. Case questions and assessment set the stage for individual or group dialog and reflection in order to improve situational awareness and understanding, identify significant force protection issues, and learn from operational observations and after action critiques. Assessment can suggest ways to remedy readiness shortfalls as well as reinforce effective antiterrorism applications force protection.

US Soldiers Near Kumanovo (1999)

On 31 March 1999, three US Army soldiers were captured during a NATO peacekeeping and observation mission near the Macedonian and Serbia- Yugoslavia border. Yugoslav authorities claimed that the soldiers entered Serbian territory[119] and would be prosecuted as criminals in a Yugoslav military court rather than in accordance with the Geneva Convention.[120]

The Yugoslav government exploited images of the three young men in uniform, two of them with obvious bruises and injuries, on Yugoslav television and with the international media. Soon afterwards, Yugoslavia stated that the US soldiers would not be tried and would be released at the end of hostilities. Nonetheless, a 32-day campaign of Yugoslav propaganda about the prisoners attempted to divert attention from the ongoing NATO mission to prevent ethnic atrocities in the Kosovo region of Yugoslavia. The three soldiers were released by Yugoslav President Slobodan Milošević on 2 May 1999 to a delegation of US religious leaders.

Aspects of the capture and uncertainty of hostage [prisoner] negotiations are informative for conditions that can be very similar to a kidnapping.

Region Situational Background
As a name, Yugoslavia existed since 1929 in a region formerly named The Kingdom of Serbs, Croats, and Slovenes from a post-World War I accord. After World War II, Marshal Tito consolidated his wartime partisan authority over a collection of many ethnic groups and instituted a government that progressed in its own style of communism-socialism for over four decades. The charismatic leadership of Tito and the uniqueness of Yugoslavia were inseparable in the

subsequent decades of Warsaw Pact and NATO tensions across Europe. When Tito died in 1980, Yugoslavian solidarity started to fray due to ethnic rivalries in a once unified Yugoslavia. Slovenia, Croatia, Bosnia-Herzegovina, and The Former Yugoslav Republic of Macedonia (FYROM) declared their independence in 1991. The remaining republics of Serbia and Montenegro declared a new Federal Republic of Yugoslavia in 1992. President Slobodan Milošević used coercion, paramilitary, and military actions in attempts to unite Serbs and neighboring republics into a "Greater Serbia." War erupted in Bosnia and regional areas suffered through massacres, mass expulsion of ethnic groups, and a resulting mass exodus of refugees from contested areas.

The Kosovo region experienced similar crimes as ethnic Albanians attempted to remove Kosovo from Serbia and declare independence. Criminal actions by several factions in 1997 and 1998 indicated that a peaceful settlement was very unlikely.[121] NATO determined that additional pressure must, "...enhance and supplement [Partnership for Peace] PfP activities in both Albania and the Former Yugoslav Republic of Macedonia to promote security and stability in these Partner countries and to signal NATO's interest in containing the crisis and seeking a peaceful resolution."[122] In September 1998, NATO issued an ultimatum to stop all aggression but determined that the deteriorating regional situation required a forced peace accord.

By early 1999, continued expulsion of ethnic Albanians living in the autonomous republic of Kosovo and charges of "ethnic cleansing" by Serbs caused an international response. Some actions and reactions by members of the paramilitary Kosovo Liberation Army (KLA) rated no better in escalating incidents of murder and mayhem. In January, the US announced a plan to end fighting in Kosovo and supported NATO air strikes if autonomy to the region was not accepted by Milošević. NATO allies warned Milošević that immediate force and ground troops could be used to enforce a peace settlement in Kosovo.[123]

International diplomacy stalemated as Milošević encouraged continued acts of murder and terror by Serbian military, paramilitary, and special police in Kosovo. During March 1999, Yugoslav Army and paramilitary Ministry of Interior troops moved out of garrisons in Kosovo and about 20,000 additional Serb forces massed at the northern Kosovo border.[124] On March 24, 2008 NATO forces conducted a broad wave of air attacks against Yugoslav forces in an attempt to halt the Yugoslav offensive in Kosovo. Cruise missiles and planes attacked over 40 sites to include military sites near Belgrade.

Over the subsequent days, NATO broadened its air attacks on Yugoslavia to target Serb military forces in Kosovo. United Nations officials reported that some 500,000 ethnic Albanians had fled Kosovo. NATO officials raised the possibility of using ground troops in Yugoslavia as low-level air strikes began against armored vehicles and other tactical targets. Albania and Macedonia appealed for help as thousands of refugees fled Kosovo.

By the end of March, NATO declared that Serbs were targeting ethnic Albanian leadership for executions and the US accused Milosevic of "crimes against humanity."[125] NATO accused Yugoslav authorities of deliberate "identity elimination" of ethnic Albanians in Kosovo. Yugoslav's representative at the UN countered with an allegation that NATO was creating an "artificial humanitarian situation" in an effort to expand NATO influence in the Balkans.[126]

The   NATO   air   campaign   continued   a   punishing

offensive against critical infrastructure and Yugoslav-Serb forces. The situation along the borders of regional nations such as Albania and Macedonia remained tense. As Serb forces continued attacks on Kosovar Albanians, Yugoslavia fortified its border with Macedonia as a likely staging area for any NATO peacekeeping force.[127]

As the NATO air campaign continued to pummel targets in Serbia and Kosovo, Serbian forces captured three US soldiers by during a NATO observation patrol on March 31, 1999 along the northern Macedonian border Serbia.[128]

Previously, the US Army had been participating in a United Nations mission called UNPREDP, the UN Preventive Deployment, as a protective measure for the Former Yugoslav Republic of Macedonia (FYROM).[129] The UN mandate was essentially preventive, to monitor and report any development in the border areas that could undermine the confidence and stability in the Former Yugoslav Republic of Macedonia or threaten its territory. The mission terminated in February 1999.[130] After the UN mission ended, US Army forces remained in the area to protect US infrastructure at Camp Able Sentry at the Skopje airport. This locale would be a probable staging area for NATO peacekeepers if they were deployed into Kosovo.[131]

The three US soldiers were on a routine reconnaissance patrol northwest of Kumanovo, a town about 15 miles northeast of Skopje and the last large Macedonian town along Route E75 prior to meeting the Serbian border. Kumanovo is about 5 miles to east of the tri-border intersection of Kosovo, Serbia, and Macedonia. The three soldiers in an armored HMMWV were part of a larger three vehicle US patrol[132] that split into individual teams.[133]

The first report of the incident was a hasty radio transmission from the US soldiers that they were receiving small arms fire and were surrounded. Three grid coordinates were received[134] but radio transmissions were interrupted and no clear location could be identified by other US patrol members in the vicinity. Contact ceased suddenly with the three soldier patrol. US and Macedonian forces initiated an immediate search in the area with air and ground assets but did not find the soldiers.

Within hours, Serb television displayed three bruised and injured US soldiers captured, according to Serb authorities, in Yugoslav territory.[135] Yugoslavia stated that the three soldiers would be tried by a military court. US reaction was immediate. President Clinton stated, "Yesterday three American infantrymen were seized as they were carrying out a peaceful mission in Macedonia. There was absolutely no basis for them to be taken. There is no basis for them to be held. There is certainly no basis for them to be tried."[136]

Meanwhile, air strikes against Serb and Yugoslav forces and infrastructure continued. Targets included Yugoslav special forces, armored and other military vehicles, Serb ground forces and aircraft, and locations such as fuel facilities and a key bridge across the Danube River.[137] The NATO Secretary General reaffirmed that the alliance was determined to halt the killing of ethnic Albanians in Kosovo and to damage the Serb "war machinery" in Yugoslavia as much as possible.[138]

On April 1, Serb security and paramilitary forces attacked into southwestern Kosovo and the city of Djakovica. Reports of civilians being murdered came from refugees. Similar reports continued in the following days of April as Yugoslav forces increased the expulsion of ethnic Albanians from Kosovo, and even crossed into northeastern Albania to temporarily seize a border village.[139]

Legal status of the three US soldiers was quickly addressed by the International Committee of the Red Cross with a statement that the three soldiers qualified as prisoners of war under the Geneva Convention: "There is an armed conflict between NATO and the Federal Republic of Yugoslavia and these three captured soldiers are...prisoners of war."[140]

By early April, Yugoslavia acknowledged that the soldiers would not be tried and would be released at the end of hostilities. Nonetheless, this prisoner incident was a bargaining chip in Milošević's political maneuvering and attempts to exploit media attention while Serbs and Yugoslavs continued expulsion and terror of ethnic Albanians in Kosovo[141] and offensive military and paramilitary actions in the region.

Raid or Meeting Engagement
What actually happened near Kumanovo? As report of the capture raced throughout the international media, some correspondents speculated that the US soldiers may have strayed into Yugoslav territory by mistake. Other questions arose on why the patrol was out of mutual support distance from other vehicles in the observation mission.[142] The British Foreign Secretary stated that the US soldiers were seized in a "snatch" [raid] operation in Macedonian territory.[143] US officials were analyzing what was known of the circumstances and stated that the US soldiers had been in Macedonia when captured.

Well after the seizure and eventual release of the three US soldiers, one perspective came from individual interviews with each of the three soldiers in the open press.[144] The following narrative is a condensed and combined version of the three US soldier's experiences from their seizure by Yugoslav forces until their release over 30 days later to a US nongovernmental religious delegation.

US Army Staff Sergeant Christopher Stone, Staff Sergeant Andrew Ramirez, and Specialist Steven Gonzales were the crew of an armored HMMWV[145] in a three vehicle reconnaissance patrol. While deployed along the Macedonian border as part of a United Nations peacekeeping mission in the region, patrolling along the border had been peaceful. Local villagers usually waved and smiled as the patrols passed through villages or countryside.

When the UN terminated this mission, US Army forces remained in the region under a NATO charter. The US Army changed uniforms and vehicles representing a UN presence to the green HMMWVs and normal uniforms of the US Army in a NATO role. The attitude of villagers shifted dramatically as the threat increased of NATO airstrikes against the Yugoslav Republic. Villagers were unfriendly and even included throwing rocks at passing NATO vehicles.

By March 31, 1999, the NATO air campaign had already been bombing Yugoslavia for several days. The three vehicle patrol was conducting its regular observation mission in the vicinity of the Macedonian border. The vehicles separated to accomplish individual mission tasks in their sector. SSG Stone's vehicle was performing reconnaissance of a secondary route that the patrol might have to use for a withdrawal if Serb-Yugoslav military forces crossed the border into Macedonia. The patrol was familiar with the rugged terrain, the road network, and local villages.

As the US Army team returned from their reconnaissance, they passed through a village they had passed through at least ten times in the previous 30 days. At first nothing appeared unusual from past patrols but as they drove through the village, they noticed a military truck on the outskirts of the village. Although a truck was not expected to be in the village, SSG Ramirez thought was that Macedonians must be training in the area. The US Army team continued along the village road while maintaining some distance between the vehicle and villagers who, in the past, had thrown rocks at the vehicle.

For SSG Stone and SSG Ramirez inside the vehicle cab, the irritation of hearing rocks bounce off the HMMWV changed suddenly to shock and the instant recognition that something was terribly wrong.

Specialist Gonzales, as the gunner standing up in the turret, was first to recognize that the pings were actually rifle shots ricocheting off the armor of the HMMWV. He heard the distinctive report of gunshots from somewhere to the rear of the vehicle. As Gonzales yelled, "Down!" and ducked down from the turret, Ramirez felt the "tink-tink-tink" in quick succession against the vehicle and knew they were taking fire. Stone was thinking "Ambush!" to himself. Ramirez reacted with immediate evasive driving to get out of the zone of small arms fire.

Thinking the shooting was coming from the truck on their left they had just passed, Ramirez turned right down a dirt road. Gonzales saw Serb soldiers for the first time as the HMMWV turned. The situation fared no better as 12 to 15 Serb soldiers came into view clustered in a small group next to the road. The Serbs looked surprised. Ramirez turned the HMMWV around quickly to avoid small arms fire from the flank. Events got worse. More Yugoslav soldiers were appearing from behind rocks and haystacks. Stone remembered that moments later the vehicle was being hit with bullets from all sides.

Stone called in a situation report to his platoon sergeant that the team was under fire and surrounded. He stated the grid coordinates from the global positioning system (GPS) in the vehicle but unknown to Stone, only three of the coordinates were received. Then, the radio stopped transmitting. Afterwards, Stone reflected that the antenna may have been damaged by gunfire. In the same moments, Ramirez was attempting to get the vehicle maneuvering out of the gunfire but drove along and into a ditch next to the dirt trail. Then, the vehicle engine stopped abruptly. Ramirez believed that so many bullets hit the engine compartment that it simply ceased to function. As the vehicle wedged into a ditch, he could not get the vehicle restarted.

Serb soldiers continued to fire at the HMMWV even when the vehicle had stopped. The firing stopped and they rushed the vehicle. Both the US soldiers and Serbs stared at each other and wondered what would happen in the next few seconds. Inside the HMMWV, the three US soldiers looked at each other and knew that any additional resistance was foolhardy. They had been surprised and they were surrounded. Since their mission rules of engagement directed that weapons be unloaded, any consideration to load their own weapons now was rash with about 30 Serb soldiers right outside the HMMWV.

Serb soldiers pounced on Ramirez, Stone, and Gonzales as they exited the vehicle. Five or six Serb soldiers grabbed each US soldier and started ripping their helmets and equipment off. At the same time, the Serbs were violently kicking and hitting their prisoners. Ramirez was hit in the head with the stock of a rifle that opened a gash as he fell to the ground. Soldiers kept kicking and stomping him. Later, Ramirez would learn he had broken ribs. Gonzales was kicked and beat while on the ground and was knocked semi-conscious when kicked squarely in the face. Some Serbs thought they had broken his leg. Stone received similar severe kicks and punches. The beatings stopped temporarily about five minutes after surrendering.

As the US soldiers lay on the ground among the Serb soldiers, a Serb leader directed that the US soldiers have their hands bound and brought toward the village. Villagers started to arrive and watched as the US soldiers were brought behind a horse stable. Ramirez remembered that a Serb guarding Stone had a pistol pointed to Stone's head. The Serb leader pushed the pistol away from Stone's head. Gonzales recalled being dragged around the corner of the building and hearing "...Kill you – Kill you!" in broken English from his captor.

As the US soldiers lay on the ground among the Serb soldiers, a Serb leader directed that the US soldiers have their hands bound and brought toward the village. Villagers started to arrive and watched as the US soldiers were brought behind a horse stable. Ramirez remembered that a Serb guarding Stone had a pistol pointed to Stone's head. The Serb leader pushed the pistol away from Stone's head. Gonzales recalled being dragged around the corner of the building and hearing "...Kill you – Kill you!" in broken English from his captor.

These actions occurred within the 20 to 30 minutes of capture. Stone, Ramirez, and Gonzales were loaded on the floor of a Serb truck with their hands still bound and hoods over their heads. They were transported, under guard, for about an hour over rough winding roads that eventually entered on what seemed to feel like a major highway. The truck stopped at a military site and the three US soldiers were brought to a tent for medical treatment of their injuries. Ramirez received stitches for a head gash. Gonzales' leg was inspected for a possible broken bone. All three soldiers were checked based on multiple bruises and cuts, and patches of blood on their uniforms. One of the medical people mentioned that they were prisoners of war and would be treated under the Geneva Convention.[146] They remounted the truck and were transported for about two more hours before arriving at a larger city.[147]

Exploitation and Interrogation
Stone, Ramirez, and Gonzales were separated from each other upon arrival at the city. They were interviewed individually in a press conference type of format with cameras and Yugoslav Republic civilian and military officials. They were not coerced on what to say in response to staged questions, but most of the questions were strategic issues far beyond their tactical ability to answer. Questions presented issues of international politics and policies and the purpose of the NATO air campaign. These interviews occurred within the first six or seven hours since their capture.

For several days, the three US soldiers were detained in a nearby facility for interrogation. For the first one or two days, the soldiers were placed in a chair, hands bound behind their back and a hood over their head. While waiting to be interrogated, the anxiety of not knowing what would occur next and the isolation of not being able to look around was unnerving. A guard watched them 24 hours a day. The soldiers were not allowed to speak. If a soldier moved from a specific position, the guard would kick or beat him.

By the second or third day, the soldiers were placed on their side on the floor with hands still bound behind their back, a hood covering their head, and their legs bent. They were not allowed to move. The only relief came when they would eat a meal or be allowed to use to the rest room. Even then, muscles, pressure points, and joints were very sore and cramped. Ramirez recalled the body pain of being in that restrictive position once for about a day and a half.

SSG Stone remembered the many times he contemplated whether or not they would survive their capture: "Within that first seven days, I was just preparing myself for the fact that we may not make it out of here."

SSG Ramirez underwent four to seven interrogations in the seven days at this facility. Gonzales recalled three or four interrogations. He recalled the isolation of being in the dark and not knowing if it was day or night. Ramirez tried to keep his "...head busy with data." He felt the discomfort of being dehydrated and the strain of having to hold his bowel movements for long periods without relief. By the sixth or seventh day, he hallucinated at least once and called out to a member of his unit that he thought was there to rescue him. The guard ignored him.

The three person interrogation team consisted of a man in military uniform, a woman interpreter, a man in civilian clothes, and guards. Questions were asked through the interpreter. The hood was removed from the soldier's head and he might be allowed to have his bound hands in front of him as he sat on a chair.

The interpreter and interrogators would take turns in questioning and become angry often either as a technique or from actual frustration. Even though the soldiers did not know answers to strategic questions from the interrogators and stated this to them, interrogator techniques included asking a question and yelling or banging fists on a table. Another interrogator technique was to walk slowly back and forth behind the soldier tapping on a pistol in its holster. Ask a question. Demand an answer. The movement of guards standing behind the soldier was another unsettling psychological technique. Ask a question. Create anxiety. SSG Stone remembered one guard coming up and placing a baton against his neck while another interrogator lifted his coat up to display a revolver as a threat.

Other lines of questioning sought a confession that the three soldiers were part of a US special forces unit on a clandestine surveillance mission in preparation for a NATO attack, or a team for electronic intercepts or locating downed NATO pilots. Gonzalez remembered being accused of being a spy to assist a ground war against Serbia. The three US soldiers denied all of these probes. SSG Stone was never specifically told that they were prisoners of war, but recalled interrogators saying he would be put on trial as a war criminal.

After several days of interrogation, Yugoslav authorities realized that any useful intelligence from the soldiers, if any significant information had ever existed to exploit, was now old and of no immediate value. Yet, senior Yugoslav officials realized the media attention that three captured US soldiers could still provide as the NATO air campaign increased in its attacks.

Isolation and Prison Cell
About the seventh day of captivity, the three US soldiers were moved to a prison facility. Each soldier

was placed in a separate cell about four feet by four feet by twelve feet with simple furnishings of a bed, small table, and toilet facility. Their hands were not bound and they could walk within the cell. Guards told them some basic rules on making their bed and keeping their cell clean. They were allowed to use their toilet and small wash basin as needed.

Each soldier could hear guards talking occasionally to each of the other US soldiers in their individual cells but were not allowed to say anything to either of the other US soldiers. Knowing that the other US soldiers were nearby was a consolation as the subsequent days were a period of confinement but without the physical and mental abuse experienced in the former facility and interrogations.

Release and Freedom

Unknown to the three US soldiers, in early April a Cypriot envoy attempted to negotiate their release, but was unsuccessful. By late April, a 19-member religious delegation of US Orthodox Christian, Muslim, Roman Catholic, Jewish, and Protestant leaders traveled to Yugoslavia to seek the release of the three US soldiers. Reverend Jesse Jackson, and Dr. Joan Brown as the General Secretary of the National Council of Churches, were co-leaders of the delegation. Reverend Jackson had organized the trip even though Clinton Administration officials discouraged the effort.

In the weeks of imprisonment, the three US soldiers could hear air raid sirens, planes flying overhead, and the explosion of bombs. Their only updates on events going on outside of their cells were the inflated and false claims by guards of how many NATO aircraft had been shot down. Stone remembered being told several times that the US had not requested their release. Gonzales used routines to assist in coping with the isolation one day at a time: he made his bed and cleaned his cell per the instructions of guards, walked patterns within his cell, exercised before and after his meals, prayed and sang songs to himself, and once Red Cross items arrived, played card games like solitaire.

Reverend Jackson ensured that President Milošević understood Jackson had no authority to negotiate for the US Government. Initial expectations of the delegation were in doubt with statements by the Yugoslav assistant Foreign Minister declaring that the release of the US soldiers was not "...on the agenda."[148] Nonetheless, subsequent discussions occurred between the delegation and Yugoslav officials, as well as a private meeting between Milošević and Jackson to promote the "...advantages of taking the risk for peace".[149] While Jackson presented a moral appeal to "build a diplomatic bridge," Milošević indicated that one soldier, SSG Stone, might be released. Jackson noted that with Stone being "White" and Ramirez and Gonzales being Hispanic, releasing only Stone would ". . send a very ugly signal back home."[150] Eventually, Milošević agreed to an unconditional release all three US soldiers. When Jackson received a letter from President Milošević to give to President Clinton addressing NATO conditions to stop the air bombing campaign, Jackson reaffirmed he was not representing the US Government.

In media interviews at the Croatian-Yugoslav border, the three soldiers indicated they were sympathetic with some guards on their most recent prison captivity and hoped that the two armed forces would not be forced to be enemies. Another report used terms of "...no ill will toward the Yugoslav people" and that the US soldiers had been treated well.[154] Some news media suggested that the US soldiers had started to identify psychologically with their captors in a Stockholm syndrome effect.[155]

Upon release of the three US soldiers, facial bruises and cuts form their capture were still obvious. During complete physical evaluations at a US military hospital in Germany, inspections revealed that Stone had been injured with a broken nose, Ramirez had two broken ribs and a swollen right leg. Other issues included wrist injuries due the recurring handcuff use.

SSG Stone, SSG Ramirez, and SPC Gonzales received recognition by the US Army, the United Nations, and the North Atlantic Treaty Organization for their military duty and conduct in Macedonia and captivity in Yugoslavia. The medals spotlighted the US Armed Forces expeditionary nature of their mission, their service as part of a UN peacekeeping force, their subsequent duty as part of a NATO military mission, a commendation from the US Army, their status as former prisoners of war, and possibly most significant – the award of the Purple Heart medal for wounds received in combat.[156]

President Clinton had signed an Executive Order on April 13 declaring the area around Yugoslavia a combat zone with an effective date of 24 March 1999. The area encompassed the Federal Republic of Yugoslavia (Serbia and Kosovo), Albania, the Adriatic Sea and Ionian Sea above the 39th parallel.[157]

Reviewing the details of the March 31, 1999 incident near Kumonovo soon after the release of the three soldiers, US Army officials "...concluded beyond a shadow of a doubt that they [Stone, Ramirez, and Gonzales] were abducted by forces (who were) at least dressed in VJ (Yugoslav armed forces) uniforms within Macedonia." US military officials believe that the soldiers were under observation for some time from the Yugoslav side of the border before the abduction.[158]

Tactics, Techniques, and Procedures

How "might" this raid-terrorism have been planned and conducted?

- **Broad Target Selection**

Surveyed border trace for NATO military forces working with Macedonian military or police forces.

- **Intelligence Collection and Reconnaissance**

Received regular reports on isolated small NATO units working along the Macedonia-Serbia border.

Calculated probable time-distance factors for quick reaction among small NATO observation or reconnaissance forces.

Observed actions at regular or random security routes in the vicinity of the Macedonia-Serbia border.

Specific Target Selection
Knew that size of recurring vehicular mounted patrols.

Planned probable sites for isolated contact with small NATO unit.

Planned withdrawal routes of a cross-border incursion in Macedonia back into Serbia.

Pre-Attack Surveillance and Plans
Studied the village locale near Kumanovo for a raid-ambush. Knew US manning strength and weapon systems per HMMWV.

Gained intelligence on the rules of engagement that were in effect for NATO forces along the Macedonian border.

Acquired raid equipment and material:
- Military truck
- Additional vehicular transportation (Given 20 to 30 Serbian soldiers were involved in the raid site and rapid mounted egress back to Serbia, more than one truck was required.
- Handcuffs or restraining straps
- Hoods or ad hoc material to cover heads of captured soldiers

Spoke basic words or phrases of English.

• Attack Rehearsal

Verified pre-operational checks in or near staging site.

Conducted movements for undetected passage across the border. Refined tactics of reinforced platoon-size raid.

Practiced actions for rapid withdrawal to Serbia and rendezvous at an initial safehaven or transfer point for kidnapped soldiers.

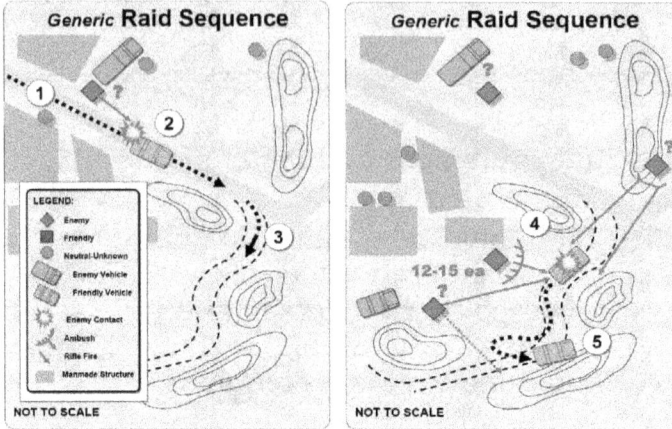

Generic **Raid Sequence**

Generic **Raid Sequence**

Reviewed contingencies for escape and evasion based on tactical conditions.

• *Actions on the Objective.*

1. Arrived at raid site and started to establish ambush attack and support by fire positions.

US patrol returning from observation and reconnaissance.

2. Initiated hasty attack with rifle fire toward rear of US patrol vehicle. US patrol attempts to evade direct gunfire and turns down dirt road.
3. Alerted raiding group elements of approaching US patrol vehicle.
4. Continued rifle fire on US patrol soldiers and vehicle as it comes upon element of raiding group.
5. US patrol turns around and attempts to evade direct gunfire

but wedges in roadside ditch.

(SSG Stone believed that a deliberate ambush was being established because the site was an identifiable location clearly in Macedonia. SSG Ramirez stated that as he attempted to evade the initial gunfire by turning the vehicle down a dirt road. The Serb soldiers he came upon were very surprised and looked like they were possibly setting up an ambush.

6. Captured and beat three US soldiers as they surrendered to raiding party.

7. Placed three US soldiers on their knees facing a wall with weapons to the back of their heads.

Continued beatings of three US soldiers.

Withdrawal

Drove in a general northerly direction along trails and undeveloped dirt roads.

8. Transported three US soldiers, bound and hooded, across the Serb border to an initial safehaven.

Arrived at initial rendezvous in Serbia with kidnapped soldiers and confirmed the status of US soldier injuries with preliminary medical checks.

Transferred US soldiers to Yugoslav military officials and interrogation elements.

9. Exploited three US soldiers on Serb television with interviews and claim of capture in Serb territory.

> **10.** Interrogated three US soldiers over first seven days of captivity in a containment facility in Serbia.

Continued physical and psychological abuse of three US soldiers.

> **11.** Relocated three US soldiers to a prison facility in Serbia and isolated soldiers from each other, news of events in ongoing NATO air campaign, and any attempt for negotiating their release.

Allowed representatives of International Red Cross to visit three US soldiers. Allowed members of US religious delegation to visit three US soldiers.

Released three US soldiers to a US nongovernmental religious delegation.

Assessment

The incident near Kumanovo was one minor episode in a much larger and long term US engagement in the region. US policy on southeastern Europe and the southern Balkans had been a significant interest for years. US ground forces experienced continuous deployments since 1993 in Task Force Able Sentry as part of a UN force in Macedonia. US Administration aims centered around three principles: support for broad European integration including NATO's enlargement, securing peace in Bosnia, and encouraging regional cooperation.[159]

At the tactical level of military operations, three US soldiers were performing their duties and abiding by their rules of engagement. A recurring observation role and reconnaissance mission, with unloaded crew and individual weapons, was surprised by an overwhelming Yugoslav military force. The leader of the three soldiers made a decision to not resist when resistance in a crisis of combat with unloaded weapons may have resulted in their deaths.

Yugoslav military forces abused their prisoners. The three US soldiers were not treated in the initial minutes, hours, and days of their capture in accordance with the protocols of the Geneva Convention for handling prisoners of war.

Yet, physical and psychological treatment varied on where the US soldiers were located and who was present as a captor. Gonzales "...saw the whole spectrum." During the first week, the US soldiers were treated very rough. Some guards presented a more soldier to soldier understanding and talked briefly with the US soldiers. Eventually, Yugoslav officials allowed the International Red Cross access to the US soldiers. Actions in the prison ranged from abusive to passive depending on who a particular guard was on duty. Some guards were professional in manner; some were not.

Once Stone, Ramirez, and Gonzales were released and in US control, the junior member of the three soldier team declared a powerful statement about unit Army camaraderie and teamwork – "I knew those guys [fellow soldiers of his unit] were doing the best they could the moment they heard our distress call."[160]

Immediate Aftermath
The NATO air campaign, Operation *Allied Force*, continued to bomb targets primarily in Serbia and Kosovo. By June 9, the Yugoslav Republic accepted a Military- Technical Agreement (MTA) that described the elements of a peace plan for the region. On June 10, the NATO Secretary-General reported that

Serb forces were beginning to withdraw from Kosovo and directed a suspension of the air campaign. Clear indications that the Yugoslav Republic was complying with the MTA prompted NATO to begin ground operations on June 12, 1999.

The UN Security Council passed Resolution 1244, welcoming Yugoslavia's acceptance of a political agreement to end the violence and rapidly withdraw of its military, police and paramilitary forces. Placing Kosovo under UN administration, the resolution authorized the establishment of a UN mission in Kosovo and deployment of a NATO-led peacekeeping force (KFOR).[161] KFOR (Kosovo Force) initiated a new phase of peacekeeping with Operation *Joint Guardian.* On June 17, 1999, NATO terminated the air campaign based on the withdrawal of Yugoslav forces and police.[162] The KFOR mission was to continue for several years.

Postscript: Milošević
In October 2000, Milošević's attempts to manipulate presidential balloting prompted massive demonstrations and strikes throughout Yugoslavia. The election winner replaced Milosevic. In April 2001, Milošević surrendered to a Serbian special police unit under a warrant alleging suspicion of corruption, abuse of power, and embezzlement. However, the Yugoslav Republic sent him to The Hague and its International Criminal Tribunal for the former Yugoslavia (ICTY) for trial on war crimes such as genocide and crimes against humanity. His trial ended without a verdict because he died during the proceedings. The tribunal issued a statement that, "Milošević was found lifeless on his bed in his cell at the United Nations detention unit..."[163] Milošević suffered from heart ailments and high blood pressure. His cause of death in March 2006 is reported as a heart attack.

Endnotes

[119] "Three US soldiers captured by Yugoslav army," CNN.com; available from http://www.cnn.com/WORLD/europe/9904/01/nato-attack.02/index.html; Internet; accessed 21 February 2008.

[120] "Milosevic may see soldiers' trial as media diversion," CNN.com; available from http://www.cnn.com/US/9904/us.kosovo.01/; Internet; accessed 24 February 2008. [121] "Kosovo: A Chronology of Crisis;" available from http://www.aiipowmia.com/other/kosovo.html; Internet; accessed 25 February 2008.

[122] NATO Press Release, "Statement on Kosovo," May 28, 1998; available from http://www.nato.int/docu/pr/1998/p98-061e.htm; Internet; accessed 25 February 2008.

[123] "Timeline Serbia 1998-1999;" available from http://timelines.ws/countries/SERBIA_B.HTML; Internet; accessed 26 February 2008.

[124] Steve Bowman, "Kosovo and Macedonia: US and Allied Military Operations," CRS Issue Brief for Congress, Congressional Research Service, July 8, 2003, 2.

[125] Ibid.

[126] "Three US soldiers captured by Yugoslav army –'Artificial refugee crisis,'" *CNN.com*; April 1, 2008; available from http://www.cnn.com/WORLD/europe/9904/01/nato.attack.02/index.html; Internet; accessed 21 February 2008.

[127] "Timeline of events - Kosovo Uprising 1998-1999," available from http://www.onwar.com/aced/chrono/c1900s/yr95/fkosovo1998.htm; Internet; accessed 26 February 2008.

[128] "US Soldiers Ambushed in Macedonia, Beaten by Serb captors," May 11, 1999; available from http://www.defenselink.mil/utiloity/printitem.aspx?print=http//www.defenselink.mil/nes/...; Internet; accessed 21 February 2008.

[129] "Pentagon: US soldiers' capture not stopping NATO bombing missions – Pentagon; Geneva Conventions cover all hostilities," April 1, 1999; available from http://www.cnn.com/WORLD/europe/9904/01/nato.attack.04/index.html; Internet; accessed 21 February 2008.

[130] "UNITED NATIONS PREVENTIVE DEPLOYMENT FORCE;" available from http://www.un.org/Depts/dpko/medals/unpredep.htm; Internet; accessed 23 February 2008.

[131] "Pentagon: US soldiers' capture not stopping NATO bombing missions – Pentagon; Geneva Conventions cover all hostilities," April 1, 1999; available from http://www.cnn.com/WORLD/europe/9904/01/nato.attack.04/index.html; Internet; accessed 21 February 2008.

[132] "Three US soldiers captured by Yugoslav army," *CNN.com*; available from http://www.cnn.com/WORLD/europe/9904/01/nato-attack.02/index.html; Internet; accessed 21 February 2008.

[133] "NATO confirms US soldiers captured, Serbian TV shows men bruised and bleeding – NATO says the 3 are missing US servicemen," April 1, 1999; available from http://www.cnn.com/WORLD/europe/9904/01/nato.attack.01/index.html; Internet; accessed 21 February 2008.

[134] Gerry J. Gilmore, "US Soldiers Ambushed in Macedonia, Beaten by Serb Captors," May 11, 1999; available from http://www.defenselink.mil/utility/pritnitem.aspx?print=http://www.defenselink.mil.news/...; Internet; accessed 21 February 2008. Major General Grange, Commander of the 1st Infantry Division comments as reported by American Forces Press Service.

[135] "NATO confirms US soldiers captured, Serbian TV shows men bruised and bleeding – NATO says the 3 are missing US servicemen," April 1, 1999; available from http://www.cnn.com/WORLD/europe/9904/01/nato.attack.01/index.html; Internet; accessed 21 February 2008.

[136] "Clinton says any trial of US soldiers has no basis;" available from http://archives.tcm.ie/irishexaminer/1999/04/02/fhead.htm; Internet; accessed 21 February 2008.

[137] "Three US soldiers captured by Yugoslav army," *CNN.com*; available from http://www.cnn.com/WORLD/europe/9904/01/nato-attack.02/index.html; Internet; accessed 21 February 2008.

[138] "NATO widens target list, seeks missing soldiers," March 31, 1999; available from http://www.cnn.com/WORLD/europe/9903/31/nato.atack.05/index.html; Internet; accessed 21 February 2008.

[139] Janet McMahon, "A Chronology of US-Middle East Relations," *Washington Report on Middle East Affairs*, Jul/August 1999; available from http://www.wrmea.com/backissues/0799/9907060.html;

Internet; accessed 21 February 2008.

[140] "Steven M. Gonzales;" available from http://www.usvetdsp.com/gonzales.htm; Internet; accessed 21 February 2008.

[141] "NATO widens target list, seeks missing soldiers," March 31, 1999; available from http://www.cnn.com/WORLD/europe/9903/31/nato.atack.05/index.html; Internet; accessed 21 February 2008.

[142] Ibid.

[143] "NATO confirms US soldiers captured, Serbian TV shows men bruised and bleeding – NATO says the 3 are missing US servicemen," April 1, 1999; available from http://www.cnn.com/WORLD/europe/9904/01/nato.attack.01/index.html; Internet; accessed 21 February 2008.

[144] "War Stories – THREE US P.O.W.s CAPTURED BY SERBS;" available from http://www.pbs.org/wgbh/pages/frontline/shows/kosovo/video/; Internet; accessed 25 February 2008. These *Frontline* interviews describe personal recollections of the patrol, initial contact with the Serbs, the attempt to evade the small arms fire and capture, the physical abuse by the Serbs, the Serb television interview, their imprisonment, and eventual release to a nongovernmental US delegation.

[145] HMMWV: acronym for High Mobility Multipurpose Wheeled Vehicle.

[146] "Geneva Convention Relative to the Treatment of Prisoners of War," United Nations, Office of the High Commission for Human Rights: As adopted on 12 August 1949 by the Diplomatic Conference for the Establishment of International Conventions for the Protection of Victims of War, held in Geneva from 21 April to 12 August, 1949 with entry into force 21 October 1950; available from http://www.unhchr.ch/html/menu3/b/91.htm; Internet; accessed 6 March 2008.

[147] SSG Stone believes that this city was Nis, Serbia.

[148] Rev. Jesse L. Jackson: Wins Freedom For American POWs In Yugoslavia," *Jet*, May 17, 1999; available from http://findarticles.com/p/articles/mi_m1355/is_24_95/ai_54796431/print; Internet; accessed 21February 2008.

[149] Susan Sachs, "CRISIS IN THE BALKANS: PRISONERS; Serbs Release 3 Captured US Soldiers,"

May 2, 1999, *nytimes.com*; available from
http://query.nytimes.com/gst/fullpage.html?res=9A05EFD8163
CF931A35756C0A96F958...; Internet;
accessed 21 February 2008.
[150] Rev. Jesse L. Jackson: Wins Freedom For American POWs In
Yugoslavia," *Jet*, May 17, 1999;
available from
http://findarticles.com/p/articles/mi_m1355/is_24_95/ai_5479
6431/print; Internet;
accessed 21February 2008.
[151] Carol Fouke and Roy Lloyd, "US Religious Leaders Receive
Freed Soldiers, Bring Them Out,"
May 2, 1999, National Council of Churches, *1999 NCC News
Archives*; available from
http://www.ncccusa.org/news/99news54.html; Internet;
accessed 21 February 2008.
[152] Rev. Jesse L. Jackson: Wins Freedom For American POWs In
Yugoslavia," *Jet*, May 17, 1999;
available from
http://findarticles.com/p/articles/mi_m1355/is_24_95/ai_5479
6431/print; Internet;
accessed 21 February 2008.
[153] Ibid.
[154] Carol Fouke and Roy Lloyd, "US Religious Leaders Receive
Freed Soldiers, Bring Them Out,"
May 2, 1999, National Council of Churches, *1999 NCC News
Archives*; available from
http://www.ncccusa.org/news/99news54.html; Internet;
accessed 21 February 2008.
[155] Thomas Atkins, "US Soldiers Pass tests, Signs of Injuries,
American Soldiers Arrive at US Military
Hospital in Landstuhl," Bio-Yugo, Stone, Christopher J.; available
from
http://www.pownetwork.org/bios/yugoslavia/ys01.htm; Internet;
accessed 24 September 2007. The
syndrome is named after the Norrmalmstorg bank robbery in
Stockholm, Sweden in August 1973
when hostages developed compassion and a supportive for their
captors over the several day crisis.
The term "Stockholm Syndrome" was coined by a criminologist
and psychiatrist involved in the
negotiations and post-crisis analysis.
[156] "Freed US soldiers heading home with Purple Hearts,"
CNN.com, May 7, 1999; available from
http://www.cnn.com/US/9905/06/pows.return.home.02/;
Internet; accessed 3 March 2008.

157 Jim Garamone, "Clinton Signs Order Declaring Yugoslavia Combat Zone (Corrected copy)" American Forces Press Service, *News Articles*, April 16, 1999; available from http://www.defenselink.mil/utility/printitem.aspx?print=http://www.defenselink.mil/news/...; Internet; accessed 21 February 2008.

158 "Freed US soldiers heading home with Purple Hearts," *CNN.com*, May 7, 1999; available from http://www.cnn.com/US/9905/06/pows.return.home.02/; Internet; accessed 3 March 2008. As late as 2003, the former US Army division commander of Stone, Ramirez, and Gonzales stated that, "Three of our soldiers were taken prisoner in Macedonia during the Kosovo campaign and taken into Serbia, and were held for awhile until eventually they were released. See "Grange: Treatment of POWs was a violation," *CNN.com*, March 25, 2003; available from http://editon.cnn.hu/2003/US/03/23/sprj.irq.general.grange.pow/index.html; Internet; accessed 25 February 2008.

159 Julie Kim, "Macedonia: Conflict Spillover Prevention," *CRS Report for Congress*, July 23,1998, Congressional Research Service - The Library of Congress, 5.

160 "Freed US soldiers heading home with Purple Hearts," *CNN.com*, May 7, 1999; available from http://www.cnn.com/US/9905/06/pows.return.home.02/; Internet; accessed 3 March 2008.

161"Kosovo – timeline of events;" available from http://www.balkantimes.com/cocoon/setimes/xhtml/en_GB/features/setimes/special/kosovo/contexts/t imeline; Internet; accessed 26 February 2008.

162 Steve Bowman, "Kosovo and Macedonia: US and Allied Military Operations," July 8, 2003, *CRS Issue Brief for Congress*, Congressional Research Service - The Library of Congress, 5 and 6.

163 Phillipe Naughton, "Slobodan Milosevic dies," March 11, 2006; available from http://www.timeslonline.co.uk/tol/news/world/article740089.ece; Internet; accessed 21 February 2008.

CRITICAL THINKING EXERCISE

I recall this incident very clearly. I was in the former Yugoslavia working for the United Nations as an international war crimes investigator when this went down. While there are a number of errors in the article related to the political complexities of the region and the application of the Geneva Conventions of 1949, the U.S. Army nevertheless accurately depicts the security situation through an excellent case-study approach. Assuming that the brave and fiercely loyal U.S. soldiers were in Macedonia when taken into custody by Serb forces, describe in detail what went wrong, what the soldiers should not have done, and what they did correctly in such a tough situation. The aim here, as the U.S. Army has done, is to provide a venue to for an after-action review and a means for lessons learned.

Into the War Theater
An Inside Look at Special Training

FBI Law Enforcement Bulletin

05/28/10

W HEN SPECIAL AGENT RICK M. DEPLOYED TO Afghanistan for temporary duty in 2004, only a handful of FBI personnel were assigned to the war theater, and the Bureau had no formal training program to prepare them for the experience.

Today, much has changed. Hundreds of our agents, analysts, and support staff have volunteered for assignments in Afghanistan and Iraq, and Agent M.— who has returned overseas several times since his first trip—is one of the people in charge of their pre-deployment training.

Now, all FBI personnel going to Afghanistan and Iraq— with assignments ranging from four months to a year—attend an intensive two-week training program to prepare them for what the military calls the "non-permissive environment" they will encounter.

FBI.gov attended a recent training class in Utah, and over the next several weeks—with articles, pictures, and video—we will report on the training, the veteran instructors who administer it, and the "students" who will soon be using their new knowledge in-country to support a variety of FBI missions.

"We base the training in Utah—especially in the remote mountains around Salt Lake City—because the area is similar to conditions in Afghanistan," Agent M. said. "The climate, elevation, and topography are in many ways the same."

Run by our International Operations Division, the pre-deployment program consists of indoor classroom training—everything from administrative details about visas and passports to briefings on insurgency activity—as well as outdoor instruction in Utah's harsh winter climate at nearly 6,000 feet above sea level.

Classes include hands-on weapons training, land navigation techniques, and emergency trauma medicine. "We go through a lot of fake blood," said Agent M., one of the program's four coordinators. He added that the 12 consecutive days of rigorous instruction is "like taking a drink from a fire hose," but there is no other alternative.

"To try to train somebody overseas—when they've just traveled on an airplane for 30 hours, are sleep deprived, and are under real-world stress—is not really an option," he explained. "What we strive for with pre-deployment training is that you shouldn't see or hear anything in country that you haven't already seen or heard here first."

When Agent M. first went to Afghanistan, the few agents there mostly provided expertise to the military. But now, working through our legal attaché program in coordination with the governments of Afghanistan and Iraq, the Bureau is involved with just about every kind of investigation in the war theater that we carry out domestically, from public corruption and kidnapping cases to terrorism and weapons of mass destruction matters.

"We've given this training to agents, analysts, linguists, IT specialists—you name the discipline, they've come through the class," he said.

Since the pre-deployment program was officially established at the end of 2004, hundreds of Bureau personnel have benefited from the instruction.

"For the FBI folks who raise their hand to go into a war zone," Agent M. said, "we owe it to them to provide the most applicable and relevant training possible prior to their deployment."

The conference room in our Salt Lake City Field Office was filled with FBI employees who had traveled from around the country to be there. The nearly 70 men and women assembled had a variety of different skills and backgrounds, but they all shared one thing in common—they would soon be deploying to a war zone.

One of the first orders of business was for everyone to stand up, introduce themselves, and explain where they would be going and what job they would be doing there. The responses were testimony to our expanding role in the war theater.

One by one, special agents, intelligence analysts, and other support employees—all of whom had volunteered—described their assignments and their specialties: analysts collecting intelligence on terrorist networks, investigators heading to our task forces on major crimes and corruption, and Evidence Response Team members, polygraph examiners, bomb techs, Human Intelligence officers, biometrics experts, and others who would be involved in counterterrorism work too sensitive to mention.

"The terrorists are planning and plotting," James McTighe, special agent in charge of our Salt Lake City office, told the group. "And make no mistake: they will continue their concerted efforts to kill our people. That's why your jobs on the front lines of the war zone—at the tip of the spear—are so critical."

"You are going to be in a dangerous place," added Special Agent Pete O., a veteran of multiple overseas deployments and one of the training program's managers. "But it will also be one of the most satisfying missions you will ever undertake for the Bureau."

Throughout the day, students received briefings from a variety of instructors who had been to the war zone and could speak from experience. There was no sugar-coating about how difficult and demanding conditions could be.

Afghanistan—about the size of Texas—is not only dangerous because of terrorists and suicide bombers. Mountain ranges rise more than 20,000 feet above sea level while summer temperatures in the desert regularly exceed 110 degrees. And because the country lacks modern amenities, the threat of diseases like tuberculosis and hepatitis can be just as deadly as enemy fire.

Instructional components would move from classroom presentations to practice drills to outdoor role-playing scenarios with more stress and complexity progressively added at each level. Some of those scenarios—drawn from real situations—would include simulated al Qaeda and Taliban attacks complete with realistic facsimiles of improvised explosives devices, rocket propelled grenades, and small-arms fire.

"Our FBI personnel overseas are going to be working long hours, seven days a week," said Special Agent Dave S., one of the program's managers. "This training is only two weeks, but it's rigorous and demanding—both mentally and physically. We hope our people will never have to contend with the situations they will face in training," he added, "but we are preparing them in case they do."

Into the War Theater -- Learning How to Save Lives

06/08/10

High in the rugged mountains outside Salt Lake City, FBI personnel preparing for assignments in Iraq and Afghanistan took their seats at rows of long tables inside a no-frills training facility and studied the first aid kits and CPR dummies in front of them. They were about to get a crash course in how to save a life.

"During the next few days we are going to give you valuable information we hope you never have to use." Tactical combat casualty care—far more advanced than routine first aid techniques—is an essential component of pre-deployment training. Students learn how to apply tourniquets, open airways, and quickly assess and treat serious injuries under battlefield conditions.

"If you're driving in Kabul and your vehicle is blown up by an IED, you don't have to be a doctor or have one there to keep someone alive until help comes," Vecchio said.

The medical training is so realistic that students learning how to properly insert a needle to re-inflate a collapsed lung could feel actual tissue and bone because instructors inserted a rack of raw beef ribs inside the chest cavity of one of the plastic dummies.

As they practiced using tourniquets in a quiet, lighted classroom, some students were surprised to hear one instructor's guarantee that before the training was over, they would accomplish the same task with one hand, in the dark, while under simulated enemy attack—and be able to do it in a matter of seconds.

"Right now," said Special Agent Dave S., one of the training program's managers, "we're crawling, learning basic principles like putting on a tourniquet, putting on a splint, checking airways. As we add layers of complexity and more stress to the drills, that's when we 'walk' and ultimately 'run'."

"Walking"—and some dragging—began the next day on a cold and snowy morning. The class spent most of the day outside, repeating a variety of drills to hone their new skills. Some of those skills were being practiced on 185-pound, full-sized dummies. Often, the dummies needed to be dragged, sometimes by only one person, from attack scenarios to safety before teams could assess and treat their injuries.

In a war zone, the tactical aspect of trauma care is critical. Before being able to rescue and treat the wounded, students learned how to keep themselves safe by establishing a security perimeter and laying down suppressive fire if necessary. As everyone took turns being the lead medic or team leader, instructors—doctors and experienced combat medics themselves—monitored all the action, offering advice and providing additional challenges.

If a tourniquet was not put on a dummy correctly or an injury was missed during the assessment phase, instructors would keep squirting blood around the wound until the correct care was given—only then would the "bleeding" stop.

"Next week we'll put students in an even more stressful environment, with people shooting at them," Agent S. said. "We keep applying stress so that they can repeat these techniques instinctively. In an emergency situation," he added, "a few seconds can mean the difference between life and death."

Into the War Theater -- Making a Contribution

07/01/10

Special Agent Pat S. stood before the pre-deployment training class and spoke in great detail about our counterterrorism operations in Afghanistan. He wasn't using notes because the material was fresh in his mind—it had been only 10 days since he returned from Kabul.

"Less than two weeks after a four-and-a-half-month deployment, I was able to give our people almost real-time information about the counterterrorism mission in Afghanistan," he said. "The environment there changes very rapidly, so to be able to provide that kind of current information is very valuable."

One of the strengths of the pre-deployment training course is that most of the instructors—and everyone who manages the program—have had firsthand experience in the war zone and can offer "ground truth" to those who are about to deploy.

Agent S., who served as an assistant legal attaché in Kabul during his most recent deployment, reiterated what many had said before him about conditions in Afghanistan—the air quality is poor, the food can be dicey, and Bureau personnel there regularly work long hours seven days a week. "But there's no question," he added, "that this assignment has been the best in my career and given me the highest sense of accomplishment. Many of my peers feel the same way."

When the 9/11 attacks occurred, Agent S. was working narcotics cases on a task force in New York City. The task force office, located near the World Trade Center, was destroyed during the attacks. "From that point forward," he said, "I felt a very strong sense of purpose about our counterterrorism mission and have been working Afghanistan and Pakistan matters ever since."

Many in the pre-deployment training class volunteered for war-theater assignments for similar reasons. "If you work counterterrorism," one agent said, "that's where you can make a major contribution."

Some younger analysts and agents who joined the Bureau after 9/11 said they felt it was their patriotic duty to volunteer for assignments in Iraq and Afghanistan. Others in the class have children currently serving overseas in the armed forces and want to support the military's efforts. One agent said he volunteered in the hopes that his work might help hasten the day when all our troops could come home.

"In a variety of ways," Agent S. said, "there is a significant opportunity for our people to contribute in theater to help protect the lives of soldiers and other Americans, Western interests, as well as Afghans or Iraqis."

Special Agent Rick M., one of the pre-deployment training program's managers and a veteran of multiple deployments to Afghanistan, put it another way: "All of us become FBI agents because we want to make an impact and serve our country. This is a great opportunity for our people to get experience on the front lines of the counterterrorism mission."

Agent S. found the pre-deployment training very helpful in that regard. "When you have already mentally rehearsed all these scenarios, heard the military terminology, and have an idea of what the daily tempo will be like, it's a lot less you have to learn when you get there."

Into the War Theater -- Staying Out of Harm's Way

07/06/10
The two-car convoy was moving slowly down a narrow mountain road when suddenly there was a loud bang. An explosion struck the first vehicle, and it was immediately enveloped by smoke.

Realizing that the first vehicle had been hit by an improvised explosive device (IED), agents in the second car prepared to get their wounded teammates to safety—but they soon had problems of their own. Emerging from their SUV, they were ambushed from the tree line. Small-arms fire in the form of bright red and yellow paintballs pelted the doors and windows of both vehicles, and the agents were forced to take cover and return fire before trying to rescue the injured.

The IED, though loud and smoky, was simulated, and the paintballs were not deadly—although they could easily raise a stinging welt on the skin. But the scenario along that narrow mountain road was real enough: the convoy was under attack and in trouble.

In the war theater, there is no telling how or when the enemy might mount an attack. It could be an IED or a sniper ambush. It might be planned in advance or a spur-of-the-moment assault. Either way, knowing how to react is critical to surviving.

"First and foremost, we teach our people how to stay out of harm's way," said Special Agent Rick M., one of the pre-deployment training program managers. "But because we are operating in a war zone, we also train for worst-case scenarios."

The best way to stay safe is by exercising situational awareness—assessing and understanding your surroundings at all times. During the training program, instructors, some fresh from in-country deployments, offered firsthand information to students on how to avoid dangerous situations and how to react if attacked. Real-world examples from Iraq and Afghanistan—some with deadly outcomes—underscored the importance of these lessons.

"If you find yourself in danger or under attack," Agent M. said, "the first rule is to react quickly and get out of harm's way."

The convoy attack and several other scenarios that were run on the next-to-last day of the pre-deployment course combined all the medical, firearms, and tactical training students had learned during the program. Now their skills were being put to the test under the most difficult of circumstances.

"If you come under attack," Agent M. said, "you know you have to act, but you need to remember everything that you're supposed to do. You have all your equipment that you must maintain possession of and not leave behind. You have your fellow agents in your car, some of whom may be wounded, and you have people in the woods shooting at you. It's a difficult situation."

After each scenario, instructors briefed students on what they did well and where there was room for improvement. In two short weeks, the class had gained an impressive set of skills—knowledge that could save their lives or help them save someone else's life.

"The whole point of pre-deployment training," Agent M. said, "is that when our people go into theater, they can deal with whatever situation is presented and get out as safely as possible with everybody intact. Safety is always our primary goal."

DISCUSSION QUESTION

Sending civilians into war zones is a tough job—even when they are armed. The FBI has certainly done the right thing by providing this training to their personnel. As well as they are trained for domestic law enforcement, working in hostile environments raises the bar to another league altogether.

While this short article can hardly describe all necessary training, I have noticed one glaring omission. After having worked in war zones for a number of years as an international war crimes investigator, there is an area of preparation that is not mentioned here. What do you think it might be? One clue: It has to do with human behavior.

Additionally, when undertaking threat assessments in war zones, there is a notion known as "reverse engineering" that is applicable. What do you think this means in this situation?

United Nations   **A/RES/49/59**

General Assembly

Distr. GENERAL

9 December 1994

ORIGINAL:
ENGLISH

A/RES/49/59

84th plenary meeting
9 December 1994

CONVENTION ON THE SAFETY OF THE
UNITED NATIONS AND ASSOCIATED PERSONNEL

THE GENERAL ASSEMBLY,

Considering that the codification and progressive development of international law contributes to the implementation of the purposes and principles set forth in Articles 1 and 2 of the Charter of the United Nations,

Gravely concerned at the increasing number of attacks on United Nations and associated personnel that have caused death or serious injury,

Bearing in mind that United Nations operations may be conducted in situations that entail risk to the safety of United Nations and associated personnel,

Recognizing the need to strengthen and to keep under review arrangements for the protection of United Nations and associated personnel,

Recalling its resolution 48/37 of 9 December 1993, by which it established the Ad Hoc Committee on the Elaboration of an International Convention Dealing with the Safety and Security of United Nations and Associated Personnel, with particular reference to responsibility for attacks on such personnel,

Taking into account the report of the Ad Hoc Committee, in particular the revised negotiating text resulting from the work of the Ad Hoc Committee,

Recalling its decision, in accordance with the recommendation of the Ad Hoc Committee, to re-establish, at its current session, a working group within the framework of the Sixth Committee to continue consideration of the revised negotiating text and of proposals relating thereto,

Having considered the text of the draft convention prepared by the working group and submitted to the Sixth Committee for consideration with a view to its adoption,

1. Adopts and opens for signature and ratification, acceptance or approval, or for accession, the Convention on the Safety of United Nations and Associated Personnel, the text of which is annexed to the present resolution;

2. Urges States to take all appropriate measures to ensure the safety and security of United Nations and associated personnel within their territory;

3. Recommends that the safety and security of United Nations and associated personnel be kept under continuing review by all relevant bodies of the Organization;

4. Underlines the importance it attaches to the speedy conclusion of a comprehensive review of arrangements for compensation for death, disability, injury or illness attributable to peace-keeping service, with a view to developing equitable and appropriate arrangements and to ensuring expeditious reimbursement.

ANNEX

CONVENTION ON THE SAFETY OF THE UNITED NATIONS AND ASSOCIATED PERSONNEL

THE STATES PARTIES TO THIS CONVENTION,

Deeply concerned over the growing number of deaths and injuries resulting from deliberate attacks against United Nations and associated personnel,

Bearing in mind that attacks against, or other mistreatment of, personnel who act on behalf of the United Nations are unjustifiable and unacceptable, by whomsoever committed,

Recognizing that United Nations operations are conducted in the common interest of the international community and in accordance with the principles and purposes of the Charter of the United Nations,

Acknowledging the important contribution that United Nations and associated personnel make in respect of United Nations efforts in the fields of preventive diplomacy, peacemaking, peace-keeping, peace-building and humanitarian and other operations,

Conscious of the existing arrangements for ensuring the safety of United Nations and associated personnel, including the steps taken by the principal organs of the United Nations, in this regard,

Recognizing none the less that existing measures of protection for United Nations and associated personnel are inadequate,

Acknowledging that the effectiveness and safety of United Nations operations are enhanced where such operations are conducted with the consent and cooperation of the host State,

Appealing to all States in which United Nations and associated personnel are deployed and to all others on whom such personnel may rely, to provide comprehensive support aimed at facilitating the conduct and fulfilling the mandate of United Nations operations,

Convinced that there is an urgent need to adopt appropriate and effective measures for the prevention of attacks committed against United Nations and associated personnel and for the punishment of those who have committed such attacks,

Have agreed as follows:

Article 1

Definitions

For the purposes of this Convention:

(a) "United Nations personnel" means:

(i) Persons engaged or deployed by the Secretary-General of the United Nations as members of the military, police or civilian components of a United Nations operation;

(ii) Other officials and experts on mission of the United Nations or its specialized agencies or the International Atomic Energy Agency who are present in an official capacity in the area where a United Nations operation is being conducted;

(b) "Associated personnel" means:

(i) Persons assigned by a Government or an intergovernmental organization with the agreement of the competent organ of the United Nations;

(ii) Persons engaged by the Secretary-General of the United Nations or by a specialized agency or by the International Atomic Energy Agency;

(iii) Persons deployed by a humanitarian non-governmental organization or agency under an agreement with the Secretary-General of the United Nations or with a specialized agency or with the International Atomic Energy Agency, to carry out activities in support of the fulfilment of the mandate of a United Nations operation;

(c) "United Nations operation" means an operation established by the competent organ of the United Nations in accordance with the Charter of the United Nations and conducted under United Nations authority and control:

(i) Where the operation is for the purpose of maintaining or restoring international peace and security; or

(ii) Where the Security Council or the General Assembly has declared, for the purposes of this Convention, that there exists an exceptional risk to the safety of the personnel participating in the operation;

(d) "Host State" means a State in whose territory a United Nations operation is conducted;

(e) "Transit State" means a State, other than the host State, in whose territory United Nations and associated

personnel or their equipment are in transit or temporarily present in connection with a United Nations operation.

Article 2

Scope of application

1. This Convention applies in respect of United Nations and associated personnel and United Nations operations, as defined in article 1.

2. This Convention shall not apply to a United Nations operation authorized by the Security Council as an enforcement action under Chapter VII of the Charter of the United Nations in which any of the personnel are engaged as combatants against organized armed forces and to which the law of international armed conflict

applies.

Article 3

Identification

1. The military and police components of a United Nations operation and their vehicles, vessels and aircraft shall bear distinctive identification. Other personnel, vehicles, vessels and aircraft involved in the United Nations operation shall be appropriately identified unless otherwise decided by the Secretary-General of the United Nations.

2. All United Nations and associated personnel shall carry appropriate identification documents.

Article 4

Agreements on the status of the operation

The host State and the United Nations shall conclude as soon as possible an agreement on the status of the United Nations operation and all personnel engaged in the operation including, inter alia, provisions on privileges and immunities for military and police components of the operation.

Article 5

Transit

A transit State shall facilitate the unimpeded transit of United Nations and associated personnel and their equipment to and from the host State.

Article 6

Respect for laws and regulations

1. Without prejudice to such privileges and immunities as they may enjoy or to the requirements of their duties, United Nations and associated personnel shall:

(a) Respect the laws and regulations of the host State and the transit State; and

(b) Refrain from any action or activity incompatible with the impartial and international nature of their duties.

2. The Secretary-General of the United Nations shall take all appropriate measures to ensure the observance of these obligations.

Article 7

Duty to ensure the safety and security of United Nations and associated personnel

1. United Nations and associated personnel, their equipment and premises shall not be made the object of attack or of any action that prevents them from discharging their mandate.

2. States Parties shall take all appropriate measures to ensure the safety and security of United Nations and associated personnel. In particular, States Parties shall take all appropriate steps to protect United Nations and associated personnel who are deployed in their territory from the crimes set out in article 9.

3. States Parties shall cooperate with the United Nations and other States Parties, as appropriate, in the implementation of this Convention, particularly in any case where the host State is unable itself to take the required measures.

Article 8

Duty to release or return United Nations and associated personnel captured or detained

Except as otherwise provided in an applicable status-of-forces agreement, if United Nations or associated personnel are captured or detained in the course of the performance of their duties and their identification has been established, they shall not be subjected to interrogation and they shall be promptly released and returned to United Nations or other appropriate authorities. Pending their release such personnel shall be treated in accordance with universally recognized standards of human rights and the principles and spirit of the Geneva Conventions of 1949.

Article 9

Crimes against United Nations and associated personnel

1. The intentional commission of:

(a) A murder, kidnapping or other attack upon the person or liberty of any United Nations or associated personnel;

(b) A violent attack upon the official premises, the private accommodation or the means of transportation of any United Nations or associated personnel likely to endanger his or her person or liberty;

(c) A threat to commit any such attack with the objective of compelling a physical or juridical person to do or to refrain from doing any act;

(d) An attempt to commit any such attack; and

(e) An act constituting participation as an accomplice in any such attack, or in an attempt to commit such attack, or in organizing or ordering others to commit such attack, shall be made by each State Party a crime under its national law.

2. Each State Party shall make the crimes set out in paragraph 1 punishable by appropriate penalties which shall take into account their grave nature.

Article 10

Establishment of jurisdiction

1. Each State Party shall take such measures as may be necessary to establish its jurisdiction over the crimes set out in article 9 in the following cases:

(a) When the crime is committed in the territory of that State or on board a ship or aircraft registered in that State;

(b) When the alleged offender is a national of that State.

2. A State Party may also establish its jurisdiction over any such crime when it is committed:

(a) By a stateless person whose habitual residence is in that State; or

(b) With respect to a national of that State; or

(c) In an attempt to compel that State to do or to abstain from doing any act.

3. Any State Party which has established jurisdiction as mentioned in paragraph 2 shall notify the Secretary-General of the United Nations. If such State Party subsequently rescinds that jurisdiction, it shall notify the Secretary-General of the United Nations.

4. Each State Party shall take such measures as may be necessary to establish its jurisdiction over the crimes

set out in article 9 in cases where the alleged offender is present in its territory and it does not extradite such person pursuant to article 15 to any of the States Parties which have established their jurisdiction in accordance with paragraph 1 or 2.

5. This Convention does not exclude any criminal jurisdiction exercised in accordance with national law.

Article 11

Prevention of crimes against United Nations and associated personnel

States Parties shall cooperate in the prevention of the crimes set out in article 9, particularly by:

(a) Taking all practicable measures to prevent preparations in their respective territories for the commission of those crimes within or outside their territories; and

(b) Exchanging information in accordance with their national law and coordinating the taking of administrative and other measures as appropriate to prevent the commission of those crimes.

Article 12

Communication of information

1. Under the conditions provided for in its national law, the State Party in whose territory a crime set out in article 9 has been committed shall, if it has reason to believe that an alleged offender has fled from its territory, communicate to the Secretary-General of the United Nations and, directly or through the Secretary-General, to the State or States concerned all the pertinent facts regarding the crime committed and all available information regarding the identity of the

alleged offender.

2. Whenever a crime set out in article 9 has been committed, any State Party which has information concerning the victim and circumstances of the crime shall endeavour to transmit such information, under the conditions provided for in its national law, fully and promptly to the Secretary-General of the United Nations and the State or States concerned.

Article 13

Measures to ensure prosecution or extradition

1. Where the circumstances so warrant, the State Party in whose territory the alleged offender is present shall take the appropriate measures under its national law to ensure that person's presence for the purpose of prosecution or extradition.

2. Measures taken in accordance with paragraph 1 shall be notified, in conformity with national law and without delay, to the Secretary-General of the United Nations and, either directly or through the Secretary-General, to:

(a) The State where the crime was committed;

(b) The State or States of which the alleged offender is a national or, if such person is a stateless person, in whose territory that person has his or her habitual residence;

(c) The State or States of which the victim is a national; and

(d) Other interested States.

Article 14

Prosecution of alleged offenders

The State Party in whose territory the alleged offender is present shall, if it does not extradite that person, submit, without exception whatsoever and without undue delay, the case to its competent authorities for the purpose of prosecution, through proceedings in accordance with the law of that State. Those authorities shall take their decision in the same manner as in the case of an ordinary offence of a grave nature under the law of that State.

Article 15

Extradition of alleged offenders

1. To the extent that the crimes set out in article 9 are not extraditable offences in any extradition treaty existing between States Parties, they shall be deemed to be included as such therein. States Parties undertake to include those crimes as extraditable offences in every extradition treaty to be concluded between them.

2. If a State Party which makes extradition conditional on the existence of a treaty receives a request for extradition from another State Party with which it has no extradition treaty, it may at its option consider this Convention as the legal basis for extradition in respect of those crimes. Extradition shall be subject to the conditions provided in the law of the requested State.

3. States Parties which do not make extradition conditional on the existence of a treaty shall recognize those crimes as extraditable offences between themselves subject to the conditions provided in the law of the requested State.

4. Each of those crimes shall be treated, for the purposes of extradition between States Parties, as if it had been committed not only in the place in which it occurred but also in the territories of the States Parties which have established their jurisdiction in accordance with paragraph 1 or 2 of article 10.

Article 16

Mutual assistance in criminal matters

1. States Parties shall afford one another the greatest measure of assistance in connection with criminal proceedings brought in respect of the crimes set out in article 9, including assistance in obtaining evidence at their disposal necessary for the proceedings. The law of the requested State shall apply in all cases.

2. The provisions of paragraph 1 shall not affect obligations concerning mutual assistance embodied in any other treaty.

Article 17

Fair treatment

1. Any person regarding whom investigations or proceedings are being carried out in connection with any of the crimes set out in article 9 shall be guaranteed fair treatment, a fair trial and full protection of his or her rights at all stages of the investigations or proceedings.

2. Any alleged offender shall be entitled:

(a) To communicate without delay with the nearest appropriate representative of the State or States of which such person is a national or which is otherwise entitled to protect that person's rights or, if such person is a stateless person, of the State which, at that person's request, is willing to protect that person's rights; and

(b) To be visited by a representative of that State or those States.

Article 18

Notification of outcome of proceedings

The State Party where an alleged offender is prosecuted shall communicate the final outcome of the proceedings to the Secretary-General of the United Nations, who shall transmit the information to other States Parties.

Article 19

Dissemination

The States Parties undertake to disseminate this Convention as widely as possible and, in particular, to include the study thereof, as well as relevant provisions of international humanitarian law, in their programmes of military instruction.

Article 20

Savings clauses

Nothing in this Convention shall affect:

(a) The applicability of international humanitarian law and universally recognized standards of human rights as contained in international instruments in relation to the protection of United Nations operations and United Nations and associated personnel or the responsibility of such personnel to respect such law and standards;

(b) The rights and obligations of States, consistent with the Charter of the United Nations, regarding the consent to entry of persons into their territories;

(c) The obligation of United Nations and associated personnel to act in accordance with the terms of the mandate of a United Nations operation;

(d) The right of States which voluntarily contribute personnel to a United Nations operation to withdraw their personnel from participation in such operation; or

(e) The entitlement to appropriate compensation payable in the event of death, disability, injury or illness attributable to peace-keeping service by persons voluntarily contributed by States to United Nations operations.

Article 21

Right of self-defence

Nothing in this Convention shall be construed so as to derogate from the right to act in self-defence.

Article 22

Dispute settlement

1. Any dispute between two or more States Parties concerning the interpretation or application of this Convention which is not settled by negotiation shall, at the request of one of them, be submitted to arbitration. If within six months from the date of the request for arbitration the parties are unable to agree on the organization of the arbitration, any one of those parties may refer the dispute to the International Court of Justice by application in conformity with the Statute of the Court.

2. Each State Party may at the time of signature, ratification, acceptance or approval of this Convention or accession thereto declare that it does not consider itself bound by all or part of paragraph 1. The other States Parties shall not be bound by paragraph 1 or the relevant part thereof with respect to any State Party which has made such a reservation.

3. Any State Party which has made a reservation in accordance with paragraph 2 may at any time withdraw that reservation by notification to the Secretary-General of the United Nations.

Article 23

Review meetings

At the request of one or more States Parties, and if approved by a majority of States Parties, the Secretary-General of the United Nations shall convene a meeting of the States Parties to review the implementation of the Convention, and any problems encountered with regard to its application.

Article 24

Signature

This Convention shall be open for signature by all States, until 31 December 1995, at United Nations Headquarters in New York.

Article 25

Ratification, acceptance or approval

This Convention is subject to ratification, acceptance or approval. Instruments of ratification, acceptance or approval shall be deposited with the Secretary-General of the United Nations.

Article 26

Accession

This Convention shall be open for accession by any State. The instruments of accession shall be deposited with the Secretary-General of the United Nations.

Article 27

Entry into force

1. This Convention shall enter into force thirty days after twenty-two instruments of ratification, acceptance, approval or accession have been deposited with the Secretary-General of the United Nations.

2. For each State ratifying, accepting, approving or acceding to the Convention after the deposit of the twenty-second instrument of ratification, acceptance, approval or accession, the Convention shall enter into force on the thirtieth day after the deposit by such State of its instrument of ratification, acceptance, approval or accession.

Article 28

Denunciation

1. A State Party may denounce this Convention by written notification to the Secretary-General of the United Nations.

2. Denunciation shall take effect one year following the date on which notification is received by the Secretary-General of the United Nations.

Article 29

Authentic texts

The original of this Convention, of which the Arabic, Chinese, English, French, Russian and Spanish texts are equally authentic, shall be deposited with the Secretary-General of the United Nations, who shall send certified copies thereof to all States.

DONE at New York this ninth day of December one thousand nine hundred and ninety-four.

DISCUSSION QUESTIONS

Discuss how the behavioral analysis relating to violent crime and threat assessment can be used to assist the United Nations in protecting international civil servants.

23 December 2006

Security Council
SC/8929

United Nations

Department of Public Information • News and Media Division • New York

Security Council
5613th Meeting (PM)

SECURITY COUNCIL CONDEMNS ATTACKS AGAINST JOURNALISTS IN CONFLICT SITUATIONS,

UNANIMOUSLY ADOPTING RESOLUTION 1738 (2006)

Deeply concerned at the frequency of acts of violence, including deliberate attacks, in many parts of the world against journalists, media professionals and associated personnel, in armed conflicts, the Security Council today condemned such attacks and called on all parties to put an end to such practices.

Unanimously adopting resolution 1738 (2006), the Council recalled, without prejudice to the war correspondents' right to the status of prisoners of war under the Third Geneva Convention, that journalists, media professionals and associated personnel engaged in dangerous professional missions in areas of armed conflict shall be considered civilians, to be respected and protected as such.

In that connection, the Council recalled its demand that all parties to armed conflict comply with their obligations under international law to protect civilians in armed conflict. It also emphasized the responsibility of States in that regard, as well as their obligation to end impunity and to prosecute those responsible for serious violations. All parties in situations of armed conflict were urged to respect the professional independence and rights of journalists, media professionals and associated personnel as civilians.

Further to the text, the Council reaffirmed its condemnation of all incitements to violence against civilians in situations of armed conflict, as well as the need to bring to justice those who incite such violence. When authorizing missions, the Council also indicated its willingness to consider, where appropriate, steps in response to media broadcast inciting genocide, crimes against humanity and serious violations of international humanitarian law.

The meeting was called to order at 12:42 p.m. and adjourned at 12:45 p.m.

Resolution

The full text of resolution 1738 (2006) reads as follows:

"*The Security Council,*

"*Bearing in mind* its primary responsibility under the Charter of the United Nations for the maintenance of international peace and security, and underlining the importance of taking measures aimed at conflict prevention and resolution, "*Reaffirming* its resolutions

1265 (1999), 1296 (2000) and 1674 (2006) on the protection of civilians in armed conflict and its resolution 1502 (2003) on protection of United Nations personnel, associated personnel and humanitarian personnel in conflict zones, as well as other relevant resolutions and presidential statements,

"*Reaffirming* its commitment to the Purposes of the Charter of the United Nations as set out in Article 1 (1-4) of the Charter, and to the Principles of the Charter as set out in Article 2 (1-7) of the Charter, including its commitment to the principles of the political independence, sovereign equality and territorial integrity of all States, and respect for the sovereignty of all States,

"*Reaffirming* that parties to an armed conflict bear the primary responsibility to take all feasible steps to ensure the protection of affected civilians,

"*Recalling* the Geneva Conventions of 12 August 1949, in particular the Third Geneva Convention of 12 August 1949 on the treatment of prisoners of war, and the Additional Protocols of 8 June 1977, in particular article 79 of the Additional Protocol I regarding the protection of journalists engaged in dangerous professional missions in areas of armed conflict,

"*Emphasizing* that there are existing prohibitions under international humanitarian law against attacks intentionally directed against civilians, as such, which in situations of armed conflict constitute war crimes, and *recalling* the need for States to end impunity for such criminal acts,

"*Recalling* that the States Parties to the Geneva Conventions have an obligation to search for persons alleged to have committed, or to have ordered to be committed a grave breach of these Conventions, and an obligation to try them before their own courts, regardless of their nationality, or may hand them over for trial to another concerned State provided this State has made out a prima facie case against the said persons,

"*Drawing* the attention of all States to the full range of justice and reconciliation mechanisms, including national, international and "mixed" criminal courts and tribunals and truth and reconciliation commissions, and *noting* that such mechanisms can promote not only individual responsibility for serious crimes, but also peace, truth, reconciliation and the rights of the victims,

"*Recognizing* the importance of a comprehensive, coherent and action-oriented approach, including in early planning, of protection of civilians in situations of armed conflict. *Stressing*, in this regard, the need to adopt a broad strategy of conflict prevention, which addresses the root causes of armed conflict in a comprehensive manner in order to enhance the protection of civilians on a long-term basis, including by promoting sustainable development, poverty eradication, national reconciliation, good governance, democracy, the rule of law and respect for and protection of human rights,

"*Deeply concerned* at the frequency of acts of violence in many parts of the world against journalists, media professionals and associated personnel in armed conflict, in particular deliberate attacks in violation of international humanitarian law,

"*Recognizing* that the consideration of the issue of protection of journalists in armed conflict by the Security Council is based on the urgency and importance of this issue, and recognizing the valuable role that the Secretary-General can play in providing more information on this issue,

"1. *Condemns* intentional attacks against journalists, media professionals and associated personnel, as such, in situations of armed conflict, and calls upon all parties to put an end to such practices;

"2. *Recalls* in this regard that journalists, media professionals and associated personnel engaged in dangerous professional missions in areas of armed conflict shall be considered as civilians and shall be respected and protected as such, provided that they take no action adversely affecting their status as civilians. This is without prejudice to the right of war correspondents accredited to the armed forces to the status of prisoners of war provided for in article 4.A.4 of the Third Geneva Convention;

"3. *Recalls also* that media equipment and installations constitute civilian objects, and in this respect shall not be the object of attack or of reprisals, unless they are military objectives;

"4. *Reaffirms* its condemnation of all incitements to violence against civilians in situations of armed conflict, further reaffirms the need to bring to justice, in accordance with applicable international law, individuals who incite such violence, and indicates its willingness, when authorizing missions, to consider, where appropriate, steps in response to media broadcast inciting genocide, crimes against humanity and serious violations of international humanitarian law;

"5. *Recalls its demand* that all parties to an armed conflict comply fully with the obligations applicable to them under international law related to the protection of civilians in armed conflict, including journalists, media professionals and associated personnel;

"6. *Urges* States and all other parties to an armed conflict to do their utmost to prevent violations of international humanitarian law against civilians, including journalists, media professionals and associated personnel;

"7. *Emphasizes* the responsibility of States to comply with the relevant obligations under international law to end impunity and to prosecute those responsible for serious violations of international humanitarian law;

"8. *Urges* all parties involved in situations of armed conflict to respect the professional independence and rights of journalists, media professionals and associated personnel as civilians;

"9. *Recalls* that the deliberate targeting of civilians and other protected persons, and the commission of systematic, flagrant and widespread violations of international humanitarian and human rights law in situations of armed conflict may constitute a threat to international peace and security, and *reaffirms in this regard its readiness* to consider such situations and, where necessary, to adopt appropriate steps;

"10. *Invites* States which have not yet done so to consider becoming parties to the Additional Protocols I and II of 1977 to the Geneva Conventions at the earliest possible date;

"11. *Affirms* that it will address the issue of protection of journalists in armed conflict strictly under the agenda item "protection of civilians in armed conflict";

"12. *Requests* the Secretary-General to include as a sub-item in his next reports on the protection of civilians in armed conflict the issue of the safety and security of journalists, media professionals and associated personnel."

DISCUSSION QUESTION

Do you believe that journalists should be afforded special
protective measures in war zones? Should there be any
limitation to those protections?

OTHER BOOKS BY DR. CENCICH

THE DEVIL'S GARDEN: A WAR CRIMES INVESTIGATOR'S STORY
POTOMAC BOOKS

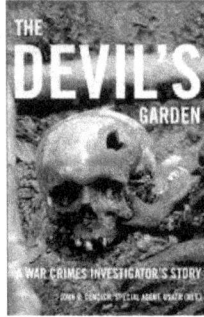

ADVANCED CRIMINAL LAW AND INVESTIGATION
THE HAGUE PRESS INTERNATIONAL

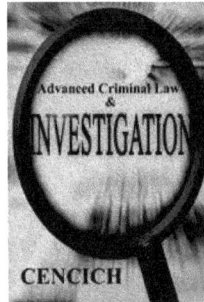

PROBLEMS IN POLICING
THE HAGUE PRESS INTERNATIONAL

www.ingramcontent.com/pod-product-compliance
Lightning Source LLC
Chambersburg PA
CBHW070356270326
41926CB00014B/2574